PASSIONATE

RELATIONSHIP

PASTOR
ADE OKONRENDE

Passionate Relationship
First published 2002
Second edition 2003
Third edition July 2019

Contact: Pastor Ade Okonrende.
Email: okonrende@aol.com
Phone: 832 723 8470, 832.372.0860

Inspiration: Holy Spirit

Chief Editor: Choice Okonrende

Cover design: Gfaydesigns
www.gfaydesigns.com 832.623.1201
Pagination: Pastor Christy Ogbeide

Books available at:choiceworldpublishers.com
Amazon.com and leading bookshops

DEDICATION

This book is dedicated:

To the glory of God.

To my mother,
Mrs. Henrietta Ojuolape Okonrende
(of blessed memory).

To my very dynamic wife, a helpmeet (my other half) who means very much to me. No success of mine is not tied to her. She was the missing link between me and my destiny. My life has not been the same since I found her — A GEM OF RARE QUALITY.

FOREWORD

This book, Passionate Relationship, is a remarkable one. It is an exciting read and yet contains some Biblical truths.

Written as a story, it includes competent counsel to parents, youth and pastors.

Guidance on the choice of a partner, valuable hints on courtship and marriage are also beautifully woven into this story where humor and profound truths flow freely together.

We warmly recommend this book to every Christian.

Pastor E.A. Adeboye
General Overseer
The Redeemed Christian Church of God

APPRECIATION

This is to express my sincere appreciation to these much beloved brethren: Sister Ronke Popoola (UK) who sacrificed her time to typeset this book from my not very encouraging handwriting.

May the Lord reward and increase Bro. Osagie Iredia (RCCG Sacramento, (USA) for typing the eighth chapter of this book.

Pastor Theophilus Martins the Managing Director of Mutual Assurances Limited, Lagos, Nigeria for his free release of his very committed and indefatigable secretary, Lawretta Obiekwunye who typed the twelfth chapter of this book and effected the necessary corrections.

Special thanks to my very much appreciated Assistant Pastor, Tokunbo Daniel of The Redeemed Christian Church of God Dublin (Republic of Ireland) who did the proofreading of this book.

A big thank you to Bro. Seyi Ilori who did the page layout of the first edition.

I am also very grateful to Pastor Ezekiel Odeyemi (R.C.C.G. Headquarters), Lagos who supervised the production of this book.

My unreserved appreciation goes to Pastor [Dr.] Christy Ogbeide who worked on the pagination of this edition.

I appreciate the efforts of my son, Choice Okonrende the CEO of CHOICEWORLD PUBLISHERS INC.

I am most grateful to my father in the Lord, Pastor E.A. Adeboye, The General Overseer (R.C.C.G.) for finding time to write the foreword to this book.

May the Almighty God bless you all in Jesus Name.

TABLE OF CONTENTS

CHAPTER ONE

BEFORE I DIE

For different cultures of the world, the birth of a female child is greeted with varying degrees of excitement or acceptance, much depends on the desire of the expectant parents.

When Tracy was born, her birth was a celebration. She was the first child of a marriage of an aging couple; they cared less about the sex of the child just as the experience of many who have probably been tagged "barren." Tracy was fondly called Baby "T" by her nurse.

Mr. and Mrs. Jackson so much treasured Baby "T" that they could sacrifice anything to keep her alive. Everyday was pleasant and fulfilling provided Baby "T" was all right. She eventually grew up to become the "obsession" of her parents. Probably due to the generous lavish of their wealth and affluence, she was over-indulged. She grew into a nice looking 'big girl,' bigger than every child of her age. She never knew pain. Her good health and happiness was the pleasure and treasure of her parent. The family doctor gave every necessary care whenever there was the least complaint on the health of "T." She was an "up-town-baby" who never knew what suffering was.

There was no doubt that "T" was growing nicely; every passing day seemed to add an inch to her height. However, she still had to learn alongside other children of her age in the nursery and Sunday school. As would be expected, her brain was developing fast to complement the physiological edge she had over her age-mates. She had a better understanding and could draw inferences from the various Sunday school lessons. To her, nursery rhymes were as simple as normal conversation. She was just exceptional. This made her a "treasured asset" of her parents.

During one of her Sunday school classes, the teacher taught the class about the life and death of Jesus Christ. She concluded the lesson with the statement, "Jesus shed His blood and died." The fact that Jesus bled to death made a very lasting impact on "T." She couldn't get over it. She grew up thinking of the statement, "Jesus shed His blood and died." You will agree with me that the Sunday school teacher was outstanding.

"T" had always been a blessed child. She enjoyed a special providence of being born on the very date of her nation's independence. She was tagged a patriot. To the family, first of October was the best day of every year, it was not only National Independence Day but also family deliverance day from barrenness. "T's" birthday eventually became a big celebration that attracted close and extended family friends. Big Baby "T" was going to be eleven years old when her overall advantage seemed to turn into a disadvantage. Everybody was getting ready for the annual happy day, the 1st of October. The proud parents had made ready new special attire for their treasured daughter. The house was loaded with a variety of food in anticipation of the usual "October crowd."

No doubt, in most cases women pay more attention to their children than the men. Mrs. Jackson was no exception. One afternoon she observed that 'T' returned from school with little or no radiance but chose to ignore her observation. Incidentally, it was "'T's" first experience of puberty. She spotted blood during break time at school. At the close of school on her way home, she discovered a "bleeding." She remembered her Sunday school lesson, "Jesus shed His blood and died." She had not the least idea of menstruation. The parents never anticipated puberty at eleven, so nobody ever mentioned anything of such, though her mother showed some concern when "T's" breasts made the first surge. It was then a laughing matter which was glossed over. All big Baby "T" was thinking of was: "Jesus shed his blood and died." She thought she was also about to bleed to death. She knew how much her parents treasured her. She couldn't imagine what life would mean to her parents should she die. This made her very sad and miserable. So difficult it was that she couldn't tell anybody, much less her mother that she was dying. She took the time to pray that the blood should stop. It was as if her prayer opened the way for more blood as she entered into the second day of her menstruation.

It was time for school, but "T" wouldn't come out of her room for fear of death that she believed would bring sorrow to her very much loved parents. Her father noticed first that she was still in her room at about five minutes past her usual departure time. All he said was "T," be sure you are on your way to school, else...!" She neither responded nor reacted. She pitied him (her father) for his ignorance of the impending "doom" (her death). 'T's" mother walked by and noticed that the driver who was supposed to take "T" to school was still waiting in the car. She was upset that "T" would get late to school if she had not left home at that time. She shouted and screamed at the innocent driver who cringed and appealed: "Madam, please tell 'T' to come out of her room. I have been waiting a long while." This was a surprise to Mrs. Jackson. She sprinted into "T"'s room."T" on seeing her much beloved mother, burst into tears. She loved but pitied her mother that she ('T ") was "going to die." Her mother screamed and asked a dozen questions on why 'T" was still indoors. She got no vocal response but "tears of pity" from "T'.

After much pressure from the mother, "T" who had padded her" flooded" newly commissioned "treasure vault" gate with many layers of kitchen roll stood up with tears profusely running down her cheeks. She hugged her mother and passionately said to her.

"Mum, it is painful that you may have to bury me on my eleventh birthday."
The mother was so shocked, she swiftly pulled her off her chest, stared into her eyes and shouted:
"You can't go." She slipped as she passed out. The driver who stood by, ran forward to offer assistance. He realized that he could neither revive nor lift Mrs. Jackson off the floor. He ran out of the room to call for more hands.

The size of Mrs. Jackson would convince anybody of the fulfillment of Isaiah 1:19: "if you are willing and obedient, you shall eat the good of the land." A few minutes after she was hauled into the car, the car sped off in an attempt to take her to the hospital. She later revived and shouted.

"T"!'T ': 'T'! Where is she?"
The driver quickly slammed on the brake and said, "Madam!
Praise God, praise God! "T" is at home."
She shouted: 'Take me back home." The driver hesitantly replied:
"We are on our way to the hospital." "What for?"She asked. The driver explained: "We were taking you to the hospital to revive you."

He was almost suffocated as she descended on him with all her weight and shouted, "Take me to "T."

Thank God for the timely intervention of her younger sister, Mrs. Thomas, who was there to accompany her to the hospital. On arriving home, Mrs. Jackson stormed into 'T's" room, held her to her chest, panting and screaming with tears, pleading; 'T" you can't do this to us. We love you. I promise you; we shall take better care of you."(In her imagination, she took 'T" to be one of those demonic children who keep appointments with death). "T" was so innocent but embarrassed, yet she could not understand how to express her experience of puberty. Her mother's assertion (as expressed in her plea) got her more confused. She felt it was obvious that she was going to die. Her mother went on to say: 'T' tell me what you need, we shall give it to you."

The innocent child was blank. Her mother ran into the conclusion that she ("T") had made up her mind to die. She wept and was compassionately joined by innocent 'T.'

The news of the commotion soon spread, and neighbors were attracted to the hubbub in Jackson's family. An old lady from the church came along and engaged Mrs. Jackson in a private conversation after seeing her and her daughter crying as they held onto each other. Mr. Jackson returning home from his work, saw more people in the compound than usual. He initially thought it was in preparation for the festive October until his wife whose eyes had become red and swollen, as she had been in tears all day greeted him. He could not understand what was going on. The wife took him aside to narrate "her assumed conclusion" about the demonic covenant their "T" had with death.

Mr. and Mrs. Jackson engaged in a discussion, which birthed a spiritual warfare prayer. The prayer lasted at least two hours. They bound all "boundables" and loosed all "looseables." They screamed, shouted and spoke diverse kinds of tongues, to make sure that they gained God's attention. There was no doubt: they were obsessed with their only daughter, "T."

Meanwhile, the old lady, who had earlier engaged Mrs. Jackson in conversation, chose to talk with "T" in a very inquisitive manner. After much persuasion 'T' decided to tell her the assumed reason why she was going to "die." She said, "Grandma, you know I love my parents. However, I love Jesus also. If Jesus shed his blood and died for me, what makes you think I will not die having shed much blood?" Incidentally, this old lady was the Sunday School Teacher who six years ago taught "T" in the Sunday school about the death of Jesus. The old lady could not come to terms with her statement. She looked puzzled and blank. At this juncture "T" said·:
Grandma (as she was popularly called in the church), see (she opened her skirt), I have been shedding my blood in the last three days. I have just decided to show you this before I die."

The experienced Grandma with surprise but a significant relief of tension was excited to realize that there was no problem at all. She embraced the ignorant little newly commissioned "Treasure-vault manager" and said:

"Praise God (the young 'manager' was embarrassed); you are not going to die. You have only become a woman." In excitement, the old lady rushed out and terminated the "prayer warring parents." She told the parents that "T" had no demonic covenant with death. It was just a display of her ignorance of puberty. The parents could not believe, in actual fact, they suspected the old lady was an agent of the devil trying to deceive them by interrupting their prayers, though they had been together in the same fellowship for more than ten years. She took them to "T" and explained the situation to both parties (the parents and their beloved daughter). Everything turned out to be a proof of ignorance.

Though 'T' agreed with the information that the shedding of blood was not going to take her life, she was not excited on her eleventh birthday. She was anxious to see the blood stopped on the fifth day as predicted by the old lady.

<u>Digression</u>

You may have to imagine various factors responsible for this clamor. Thank God ' T ' decided: "I will speak out before I die."

At this juncture may I advise you to consider the following:

1.   How you pass information to children.

2.   How you react to their expressions.

3.   Do not be obsessed by or idolize your children.

4.   Female children need more attention.

5.   Get closer to your growing baby girl so that a "strange" development or discovery will not cause you to "pass out."

6.   Educating little children on some basic human developmental processes is essential.

7.   Not all matters are purely spiritual. However, you will play safe if you approach every issue from a spiritual perspective.

8.   It saves you time and emotional stress if you have adequate knowledge of what you are praying about.

9.   Watch the signal or message you pass to children when you are in a dilemma.

10.   Positive agreement between husband and wife is a vital weapon.

11. Corporate prayer solves all problems through the intervention of the Holy Spirit.

12. Functional relationships between brethren is a beautiful asset.

Do not live in isolation: "Iron sharpens iron; so a man sharpens the countenance of his friend [to show rage or worthy purpose" (Proverbs 27:17). Speak out before you "die." Silence may cause great torture and untold hardship. However, note the person to whom you speak with when passing through a difficult time (DIGRESSION CLOSED).

CHAPTER TWO

DELIVERANCE FROM OBSESSION

Mr. and Mrs. Jackson could hardly get over their experience. They remembered it with mixed feelings. Mixed feelings because sadly it made them realize that they were obsessed with their only child. However, the experience unified them in prayer as they never ceased to engage in corporate prayers from then on. They stopped being tense and stressed about having an only child and living in fear of losing her. They learned to trust God for everything.

As the year rolled by, they decided hence-forth to celebrate "T's" birthday in "low-key." They started to enjoy God's given peace. "T" was going to tum twelve while her mother was almost forty-seven years old; her father had just clocked fifty- three a few months back.

Mrs. Jackson realized that she had not menstruated in almost two months, she hinted her husband who responded with a joke; "Welcome to menopause." They both laughed and believed that there was no more menstruation to disturb their sexual life. A week later, Mrs. Jackson felt sickly and decided to check on the family Doctor. She could hardly sense any symptoms of pregnancy because she was not expectant of anything relating to conception after twelve years of unplanned fruitlessness. She threw up at the doctor's clinic, but the experience was greeted with a joke by some of the nurses who had been very friendly with her over the years. One of the nurses jokingly said: "Madam, we shall need to order some antibiotics for you to eliminate the virus. I guess it is too late for you to have "morning sickness" now that you have gone beyond "mid-day" (referring to her age). Everybody laughed, but the doctor mused a little and said: "Let's test Sister Jackson for a "mid-day miracle." It may prove that Uncle has not "retired" from active "driving," delivery and "biological evangelism."

Everybody laughed. A clinical test was carried out; it proved that Mrs. Jackson was about nine weeks pregnant. Her size had absorbed the pregnancy (remember she eats the good of the land). She turned to the doctor and jokingly said: "Yesterday was 1st of April, please do not extend the 'April- fool' jokes".

It took the doctor some minutes to convince Mrs. Jackson that she was indeed pregnant. She turned to the doctor and the nurses around, appealing that they should not tell anybody of this "mystery." She said, "Please let it announce itself."

The discussion of the early hours of the day seemed to have triggered the mind of Mr. Jackson to a "funfair" night in the bedroom. When it was bedtime after the family prayer, he decided to question the prayer point that his wife raised at the family altar. "Let us pray that the good work the Lord has started in this family be completed. Let us tell God to fulfill His Word stated in Exodus 23:26 "No one shall suffer miscarriage or be barren in your land; I will fulfill the number of your days." EXODUS 23:26AMP

Ruminating over the first part of the prayer point, he could easily agree that the Lord had always been good to the family. He could not understand the relevance of Exodus 23:26 which reads "None shall lose her young by miscarriage or be barren in your land: I will fulfill the number of your days." On coming into the bedroom after making sure that big 'T' was in bed, Mrs. Jackson embraced her husband with a broad smile that suggested, "I want to sail." Little did he know that it was not a time to "float" as the wife whispered into his ears: "You are pregnant?"

He gently replied with a deep romantic bass "I have been"- thinking of his business plans and ambitions. The wife pushed him a little off herself as she put her two hands on her waist demonstrating pregnancy. He was stunned; the heat went out of him as he held his wife asking: What do you mean?"' His expression showed deep consternation as he squinted some creases formed on his forehead. He couldn't believe his ears, his heart throbbed. He sat at the edge of the bed as he asked his wife to "come again." She reiterated her assertion of pregnancy as

confirmed by the Doctor. Not in outright dis-belief, he embraced his wife and said,
'Let us trust God."

"That what?" She questioned.
"No... I mean you have not shown any sign of em."
She interrupted him with a song: "He has done so much for me He has taken away my sorrows, oh, glory Halleluiah..."
He baited her with a sudden shout of "Wait! Wait!! Wait!!! Is this another April fool?"

With very broad laughter, Mrs. Jackson responded:
"... exactly the question I asked the Doctor. My dear, God has been wonderful to us. The Doctor 'confirmed that I am about nine weeks pregnant." His tap of tears was opened, praising the Lord for His goodness and faithfulness. They both praised the Lord until they fell asleep. Overwhelmed, he forgot about the sexual desire, which he had nursed throughout the day. He woke up the following morning singing - "What a mighty God we serve ..." It was good news that he could not share with anybody for so many reasons: "Would they believe me?" "Is it not too early?" "Supposing it is not real?" "Should there be any problem?" "Could the devil frustrate or abort the pregnancy' He eventually concluded that "pregnancy is capable of announcing itself." ·

A few weeks later a scan test showed two baby boys. The birth of the almost identical twin was the greatest joy of the whole family especially "Big T' who felt she would be free from the false accusations of people that it was her who desired no other child in the family. Incidentally, the twin arrived September 28 just three days before 'T's"13th birthday. It was excitement galore. There was no doubt that God had shown special favor to Jackson's family. They had enough material substance to give their children the best any parent could wish for a child.

At the age of fifteen, "Sister T" as people now called her in the church was already paving her way through high school into the university. She graduated from the university at the age of nineteen. Her parents desired to hear their daughter addressed as Doctor Tracy Jackson. This she accomplished at the age of twenty-four in one of the best universities in Europe. With the help of her parents, she secured one of the best jobs in the city. To the glory of God, her success and affluence did not succeed in diminishing her commitment to Christ. She grew to become the Sunday school superintendent of her local fellowship -"A-Z Holiness Church." She rode one of the best cars in town, bought her own house but no one ever proposed marriage to her.

In her days at college, Tracy once heard her lecturer say, "Success could be very intimidating to the unsuccessful who lack personal confidence." She could now identify with those words of wisdom. Most of the men in the church were not as well-read as her; though she was not the picky type, yet very few would want to get into a conversation with her. Her exposure as the Sunday school superintendent proved to be a disadvantage as it exposed her imposing stature coupled with her excellent command of English language and sound knowledge of the word of God. Some who were jealous branded her; "show off', "too much," "Queens English." Her success intimidated some of the young men in the church. This was probably responsible for her abhorring being addressed as Dr. Tracy Jackson. She preferred being called Sister Tracy.

Tracy had always been a disciplined young lady. She was very much loved and well-guided by her parents. She never saw her father exercise strict control in the house and neither did her mum. The age gap of thirteen years between her and her "pet" twin younger brothers did not help her either. She grew up instructing the boys. She taught in the church: instructing the men. Men were subject to her on her job as a top management officer. It was a big struggle for her to be subservient to any man. Her yielding to the Holy Spirit was her greatest asset as she learned to put her personality, academics and material attainment behind her. Even though she was so friendly and respectful to men and women alike, none of the brothers in the church was bold enough to approach her for a date or talk to the Pastor on the issue of conviction for marriage.

Years rolled by and Tracy turned thirty-two. It was a tiny get-together in her well-furnished house.

There were more than enough to eat and drink for the few guests. The twin brothers were present with their friends; you can be sure they were all much younger than Tracy. Very few brethren came from the church because the occasion was not announced. Among those present was an associate pastor who was newly-wedded for less than six months. He was a medical Doctor by profession, a surgeon in the making and was posted to a nearby hospital on attachment for a period of at least six months. It was not too difficult for him to identify and associate with Tracy. He was not intimidated by her success, and more so he was married. However, he had to leave his wife at their base, which was about five hundred miles away.

The relationship between Dr. Dickson and Dr. Tracy Jackson became very cordial. He seemed to be the right type of man Tracy would like to have for a husband, but alas, it was too late. Associate Pastor Dickson was already happily married to Chimmy, a nurse by profession. They both had good knowledge of the Christian principle on holiness. They were determined to keep the purity of the spirit, soul, and body. Very soon they became fond of each other. They were always there for one another except for sex.

It became a complicated problem for Tracy to come to terms with loneliness in a big house such as hers, especially after a very cordial emotional discussion with Associate Pastor (Dr.) Dickson. On many occasions, she had returned to the house with tears in her eyes. She once wept bitterly soaking her pillow with tears asking God:

"Why me?"

"When will this loneliness be over?"

"Who and where is the man?"

"When and how will he come?"

She took her Bible and flung it open. Her eyes went straight to Jeremiah 29 verse 11: "For I know the thoughts and plans that I have for you, says the Lord, thoughts, and plans for welfare and peace and not for evil, to give you hope in your outcome " After reading it through, she added the question:

"When? When God?" she screamed.

Very soon I will be thirty-three she reiterated with a bang of her feet on the wooden floor. The vibration seemed to say almost audibly...." before then." She turned around to see if anybody was in the room with her. She saw nobody. She soliloquized: "You mean before I am thirty-three?" The phone rang. She felt. "What an interruption" as she picked the phone. She heard a voice from the other end. It seemed the person was engaged in another discussion and did not realize that he was supposed to be on the line to her house. After a futile effort, she dropped the phone. She sat down to ruminate on the coincidence of her soliloquy and "yes" from the phone. She knelt thanking God for saying I receive! I receive it! I receive it! She went to bed believing that she had had a dialogue with God. She lied down on her bed with a measure of sobriety; her countenance was suggestive of her readiness to listen to an audible voice.

================================

"Success could be very intimidating to the unsuccessful who lacks personal confidence."

================================

CHAPTER THREE

BE CAREFUL ... HOW YOU LISTEN!!!

There is no doubt that joy can be very intoxicating and contagious. Tracy could hardly sleep, throughout the night. She was anxious to share her experience with somebody, preferably, Dr. Dickson. While at work she phoned Dickson if he could come over for a cup of tea during the lunch break.

Dickson replied, 'That's no problem I am not on call today."

She felt excited as she dropped the handset. She stood up from her chair with great elation, stretched herself and swung her arms in the air as if saying, "I am liberated at last."

She suddenly heard a sound near her door; she thought to herself: "Am I becoming obsessed with Dickson? He couldn't be at the door by now."

As she moved closer to the door, she overheard a discussion be-tween two frivolous ladies. She was tempted to try and hear the subject of their conversation. As if that was going to suppress her anxiety on the expectation of Dickson's arrival. Little did she realize that it was the ploy of the devil to destroy her treasured virginity. The ladies were discussing how they had affairs with men. One of the ladies was heard to have said: Until I lost my virginity, no man seemed to admire me."

The devil straightaway planted this statement in Tracy's soul. She started thinking about her life. The devil suggested to her that it was her virginity that had repelled men from her over the years. She tried endlessly to conquer the thought with the word of God. She took her Bible and examined the following scriptures again. 1Car. 6: 19: "Do you not know that_ your body is the temple (the very sanctuary) of the Holy Spirit Who lives within you, whom you have received (as a gift) from God? You are not your own." 1Car. 6: 19:

I Corinthians 3: 16-17: "Do you not discern and understand that you...are God's temple (His sanctuary), and that God's Spirit has His permanent dwelling in you (to be at home in you, collectively as a church and also individually)? If anyone does hurt to God's temple or corrupts it ... or destroys it, God will do hurt to him and bring him to the corruption of death and destroy him. For the temple of God are Holy (Sacred to Him) and that (temple) you (the believing church and its believers) are." I Cor. 3: 16-17

"Let marriage be held in honor (esteemed worthy, precious, of great price, and especially dear) in all things. And thus let the marriage bed be undefiled;

for God will judge and punish the unchaste (all guilty of sexual vice and adulterous." Hebrews 13:4: "Therefore (beware) brethren, take care, lest there be in any one of you a wicked, unbelieving heart (which refuses to cleave to, trust in and rely on Him), leading you to turn away and desert or stand aloof from the living God." Hebrews 3:12:

"You have not yet struggled and fought agonizingly against sin, nor have you yet resisted and with- stood to the point of pouring out your (own) blood" Hebrews. 12:4

She rounded up with: "My righteousness and my right standing with God hold fast and will not let them go; my heart does not reproach me for any of my days, and it shall not reproach me as long as I live." Job 27:6

She remembered the instruction of the Lord Jesus in Luke 8:18: "be careful therefore how you listen. For to him who has (spiritual knowledge) wilt more be given; and from him who does not have (spiritual knowledge), even what he thinks and guesses and sup-poses that he has will be taken away." Immediately she felt a big relief. However, it was going to be momentary. Dickson was delayed in coming because he took an unusual route and was caught in the traffic. Suddenly as if hell was let loose, Tracy felt exceptionally sex-driven as she had never experienced in her entire life. She clamped her thighs together as if she were to prevent a man from gaining access. The Holy Spirit reminded her of Isaiah 59:19b: "when the enemy shall come in like a flood the Spirit of the Lord will lift a standard against him and put him to flight ..."

As soon as she recited this in her spirit, she shouted; "Get thee behind me Satan."

There was somebody at the door; it was Dickson. "Come in" she answered.

Dickson asked: "Was there any battle going on? I heard you rebuke the devil."

The devil quickly invaded her mind again, suggesting to her that Dickson was the only safe person who could keep the secret if she agreed to seek the "help" from him. She looked at Dickson lustfully. He got the message, though there was no verbal communication. He had a witness in his spirit that something was wrong, but it seemed beyond what he could easily handle. After some minutes of silence, she reached out to him, holding his hands and said: "You wouldn't mind my cup of tea?" What Dickson heard was "You wouldn't mind my "cup" and teat" He did not answer. After some seconds as if he was regaining consciousness he fluttered some words snappily: "Maybe later."

Tracy was surprised. She questioned: "didn't you agree to come over for our teatime together? Dickson quickly responded: "I wouldn't mind a cup of tea."

They both understood that their discussion had gone beyond a cup of tea. They felt insecure, but it was as if it was impossible for them to stay away from each other. The tea-break was over, and Dickson returned to his house. He couldn't get over what looked like a trance of an experience. He knew he was into some trouble already but felt he was strong enough to handle it. He blamed himself for many reasons, asking questions:

"Did I misinterpret her look?"

"Did I hear "cup" and "teat" or cup of tea?" "Why did I feel sexy?"

He immediately determined to avoid any further close or special visit from or to Tracy.

Dickson's departure left Tracy thinking: "Why was he lost in thought? Did he have any other thing in his mind than 'come for a cup of tea'? Would he be prepared to 'disvirgin' me if l am ready?" Suddenly she burst into laughter and said, "I will enjoy it provided he will not use a surgical knife." She soliloquized: "1 think I love him. "She nodded her head in approval.

She concluded: "It is only Dickson that can keep the secret."

She felt intimate and possessive to address him as Dickson instead of "Pastor Dickson." The day's job was over, and it was time to go to church as she did every Friday. She was to moderate the Sunday school preview for the following Sun-day service. She realized that she could not coordinate herself perfectly well. Her struggle was evident to almost every one of the Sunday school teachers. She was not her usual articulate and well-comported personality.

Her smiles were not consuming enough to cover up her inner discontentment and spiritual dejection.

It was a struggle driving towards her house; she felt a pressure in her, urging her to drive to the home of Associate Pastor Dickson. The Holy Spirit prompted her to remember I Thess. 5:22 which read: "Abstain from evil (shrink from it and keep aloof from it) in whatever form or whatever kind it may be." She also read Romans 6:12: "Let not sin therefore rule as king in your mortal (short-lived, perishable) bodies, to make you yield to its cravings and be subject to its lust and evil passions."

Right at her driveway before getting into the house, she took her Bible and read:

Romans 6:13-16, 13. "Do not continue offering or yielding your bodily members (and faculties) to sin as instruments (tools) of wickedness. However, offer and yield yourselves to God as though you have been raised from the dead to (perpetual) life, and your bodily members (and faculties) to God, presenting them as implements of righteousness, 14: For sin shall not (any longer) exert dominion over you since now you are not under Law (as slaves), but under grace (as subjects of God's favor and mercy). 15: What then (are we to conclude)? Shall we sin because we live not under Law but God's favor and mercy? Certainly not! 16: Do you not know that if you continually surrender yourselves to anyone to do his will, you are the slaves of him whom you obey, whether that be to sin, which leads to death, or to obedience which leads to righteousness (right doing and right standing with God)?

She then remembered one of her Sunday school memory verses: "But (like a boxer) 1buffet my body (handle it roughly discipline it by hardship) and subdue it, for fear that after proclaiming to others the Gospel and things pertaining to it, 1 I should become unfit (not stand the test, be unapproved and rejected as a counterfeit) "1 Cor. 9:27.

It was as if a veil was removed from her face. She knew it had been a big spiritual battle.

No food was good enough. Nothing appealed to her taste. She felt lonely and deserted by everybody especially "lovable Dickson." She reverted into a "pity party": she wept bitterly, this time coupled with repentance. It was a moment God was waiting for. She received a revival in her spirit. Her experience was like nothing odd ever happened. It was a victory. She praised the Lord as she went to bed. Her sleep was a fulfillment of Prov. 3:24: "When you lie down, you shall not be afraid; yes, you shall lie down, and your sleep shall be sweet."

It was not just a sweet sleep. God gave her a revelation of who is to be her husband. Tracy had hardly closed her eyes when she found herself engaged in a very intimate dialogue with the Zonal Sunday school coordinator for the entire A-Z Holiness Church: Bro Jimmy. Jimmy was a Puritan Christian whose life- style and personal conduct had earned a tag: "Super Holy" or "What does the Bible say?" It was not unusual for any of the brethren to say: "What does the Bible say?" to caution others that their ideas may not gain the approval of the Zonal Sunday school superintendent. Jimmy, as seen in the dream (revelation), was in his unique way, very emphatic about Christian principles. His principal goal had always been on get-ting to heaven. Tracy saw him emphatically telling her: "You will not go back; you have gone too far, your fall will not be limited to only you. If it takes lifting you off the ground, we shall get to heaven together." Suddenly she found herself lifted off the ground, though without any struggle. She was restful in the arms of Jimmy who quickly ran forward through a gate; alas they were in HEAVEN!

She opened her eyes; it was but a dream. She wiped her face with both hands and exclaimed: "This is too real. "She thought in herself: "How on earth will I need Bro. Jimmy, to help me into heaven? Does that suggest any marital relation-ship? Come to think of it, Bro. Jimmy has been in courtship with Sis. Jassy, for more than a year." She concluded that it must be one of the devices of the devil to confuse her life. She never bothered praying about it.

The devil has always been known for his courage and the use of persistence to wear out man's faith and adherence to the principles of the Lord. He does not easily give up especially on those Christians whose fall will affect many others. It was a very bright and lovely Monday morning after the previous day's fantastic Sunday service that gave almost every member of the church a glimpse of heaven. Tracy was spiritually charged. She saw Associate Pastor Dickson just as one of the ministers. It was a wonderful time in the presence of the Lord.

With joy and singing, she stepped into her office, which seemed to have been turned into a battlefield by the devil. She remembered the Friday episode. A vivid picture of the whole scenario came back into her mind. She was immediately reminded by the devil that she might never be attractive to any man as long as her virginity was in place. She remembered the book of Luke 4:13: "And when the devil had ended every (the complete circle of) temptation, he (temporarily) left Him (that is, stood off from Him) until another more opportune and favorable time."

Mondays, unlike Fridays, have always been busy days. The love for her job saved her from the devil's orchestrated disenchantment against holiness. Tuesday and Wednesday were not as active as of Monday.

The phone rang. It was Dickson. He had been mandated by the Pastor to make an emergency arrangement on how to secure temporary accommodation for Jimmy, who had just acquired a new job in the city and would, therefore, need to relocate to join their local church. He saw it as big news to share with Tracy (the Sunday School Superintendent of the local branch of A-Z Holiness Church). She could probably be of help in locating vacant accommodation around town. It was a

Thursday afternoon, just a few minutes away from her lunch break. She did more listening than talking. She enjoyed hearing the voice than the message being put across. In actual fact, she was lost in thought about Dickson and her virginity. After a while, Dickson chose to be silent to get her talking. She did not say a word. Dickson thought the line was dead. He said, "hello," to which she responded,

" It's nice hearing your voice."
It was as if she did not hear all that Dickson had put across. Dickson felt he knew what was going on but couldn't be assertive. It was a very dicey issue. He wanted to play safe; he asked passionately: "Are you okay?"
The response was snappy: "Sort of."
The second telephone rang. It was a redirected call from the operator. Tracy took the phone and said, "Hello, can I help you?"
"Yes Mam, would you want to receive a call from Mr. Jimmy Davise?"

"Please tell him to call me on my direct line," she responded. She quickly told Dickson on the other line: "Please drop, there is another caller on the line; I will see you in church tomorrow." The cold attitude was of concern to Dickson who felt he must have hurt her feelings. However, he could not understand how. He felt his guess could not be right mainly because in the course of their discussion in the recent past Tracy had told him of her upbringing and strict holiness and had concluded in himself: "Sis. Tracy is a virgin."

He blamed himself for thinking that Tracy was trying to seduce him. He felt there was no ground for such suspicion because Tracy is known to be Spirit-filled. He was more confused than ever. He concluded to avoid talking to her on the phone. It seemed he heard a voice saying.

"Why should she (Tracy) be punished for your lust?" He thought it was the Holy Spirit not realizing that it was the devil trying to accuse him to get him into conversation with Tracy.

Jimmy called back as instructed by the operator, but it was before Asst. Pastor Dickson dropped the phone so that he couldn't get through. The phone rang "Hello is that Bro. Jimmy" responded Tracy.
"This is not Bro. Jimmy but Pastor King." He went on "Were you expecting a call from Bro Jimmy?"
"Yes Sir" answered Tracy, "The operator earlier redirected his call."

"Okay," responded the Pastor, "I was going to talk to you about him, but now that you are in contact, I had better allow his call to come through. He will probably tell you all I would have told you. God bless you my sister, good-bye."
He dropped the phone handset. The phone rang just immedi-ately as the Pastor dropped. This time, Tracy's response was very conventional.
"Hello, God bless you, can I help?"

From the other end came the baritone voice of Jimmy. His voice was his principal charisma. With excitement, Tracy responded: "It's wonderful to hear your voice again. He responded, "Praise God."

Jimmy narrated the miracle of his new job appointment in Dakkoma city, and how he had been mandated by his Pastor to join the local parish to which Tracy belonged. She did much listening. She hardly interrupted his testimony. She could remember her dream of almost a week ago. She was waiting for a statement that may sound relevant, but none was forthcoming. She felt that if her dream was anything to go by, she should be able to confirm through this important phone call". She was over- whelmed by her problems. She did not respond to all the stories of Jimmy's testimony except with these two words: "Praise God."

That did not sound exciting to Jimmy. After a little pause he asked;

"Don't you want me around?"

This was a very pertinent question. Tracy's response was a shocker. She said: "if l need anybody, it is you, especially at this time that I am weak."

This response was as if she demanded the master tape of what Jimmy was said to have told her in her dream. Jimmy went on to say:

"You cannot afford to be weak; you have gone too far to back out on the Lord, my beloved sister." With a tone of laughter he added, "If it takes lifting you off the ground, we shall get to heaven together."

Her only response was a loud "AMEN."

Jimmy said a short prayer and bade her good-bye. She was wordless, and for some minutes the whole environment was quiet. She reappraised all the events of the past two weeks. There was no doubt that this was a crucial time in her life. She kept thinking about the phrase... We shall get to Heaven together.

==================================

"You cannot afford to be weak; you have gone too far to back out on the Lord..."

==================================

CHAPTER FOUR

THE HEAVENLY MAN

The phone rang; it was from the receptionist, "Mam, would you like to receive any visitor?" the voice questioned.

"'Who is it?" She replied. The operator said:

"Just a second ... OK ... He signed Teddy Jackson; I guess he is your brother." "He is not my brother but my Dad," replied Tracy with a tone of offense.

"I am very sorry," the operator apologized. "Please let him in, "she commanded.

She was very paranoid about the idea of her aging look as suggested by the operator/receptionist. It was a timely visit by her father who just came to town on a business trip.

She rose from her executive chair, walked briskly to the door to let him in. They had a big hug. She dropped her head on his shoulder as she sobbed. The tears said it all. Her father held her shoulders and wiped off her tears with the fringe of his flowing gown. He said:

"I hope it's no other thing that this issue of finding a suitor?"

She narrated her plight and the way she felt about Dickson. She later confessed how she came to believe that it was her virginity that repels men from her. It was a timely visit. She couldn't have found a better person to confide in.

By the time her father finished his very explanatory sermon on holiness, the faithfulness of God and the deceit of the devil, Tracy was restored. She felt like she had always been a daughter. Her face was radiant and expressive of hope and confidence in the Lord.

"Now let me share with you why I decided to call on you without any prior notice." Tracy cut in, "You couldn't have come at a better time."

"Thank you. I believe, the footsteps of the righteous are ordered by God," he responded.

'That's true," asserted Tracy.

"On my way after my business discussion with the Bank Manager I just suddenly felt very unusually hungry. Ahead of me was a restaurant. I did not think twice before I went in there. I was enjoying my meal when a young man, at least from my perspective (compared with my age) came to sit directly opposite me. He was very polite and well cultured. The greetings from his voice were very charming and captivating. I could hardly resist granting him an audience. With my mouth full, I nodded in acknowledgment of his warm greetings. After a gulp, I responded, "It's a pleasure meeting you."

His accent was suggestive of our background, but I refused to identify with Him on that ground." Tracy cut in with some laughter:

"That is typical of some of our brethren in the church. I know a brother who has a very wonderful voice, but it seems his tongue is so set and his vocal box repulsive to change."

Her father also laughed and said,

"Let me continue with this interesting experience with this "heavenly man," I call him a heavenly man because he talked so much about heaven that I started thinking he was an angel. Initially, I thought he was going to ask for my assistance but never. With that, he eventually got 100% of my attention. I abandoned my food to listen to him. I felt so blessed by all we discussed but still found it hard to believe he was not an angel.

For this reason, I decided to ask one or two questions to probe into his personal life. I was surprised when he said he was not married yet. I thought in my mind, "that could be typical of an angel. To probe further, I asked whether he would ever get married: he smiled, and with a pause, he said "I have courted a lady for more than a year, I guess she is not heaven- conscious. She of recent told me to seek God's face afresh as she was opting for somebody else." With tears almost coming out of his eyes, he continued: "It is not her leaving me that pained me but the fear of losing her soul to the devil, as she has not shown much seriousness about the things of the Lord."

"I got more interested in this unusual personality of the century. I asked him:

"Which church do you attend?" to which he replied: "The Headquarters of A-Z Holiness Church, but I will be joining the local assembly in this city as I have newly secured a job here in Dakkoma."

To Tracy, the conversation seemed to point to Jimmy Davise, but she felt it would be rude to interrupt her Dad again. However, she realized it was not proper to listen to her Dad's story during the official hour. Her expression was suggestive of boredom. Her father paused and said,

"I guess I am disturbing your job." Her response was a very polite; "Sort of." He, however, went on to say, "Let me quickly finish my story. "The fact of it is that at the end of my discussion with this angelic personality I felt if l could help it, I would want him to be my in-law."

"And who will be the bride?" Tracy asked. Her father responded,"... eeemm well, you know, I have not two daughters but you." She laughed. Her laughter was very discouraging. He felt she regarded his long talk as a waste of time. In his frustration, he said, 'Tracy would you give me the honor of having you at a dinner on Sunday afternoon after the church service? The fact is, I have promised to meet again with this man. I did not see him eat anything throughout our discussion. His captivating voice and choice of the subject were more satisfying than any food. My principal reason was to confirm whether he was an angel or not. He sounded so spiritual, he made some categorical statements about my business experience and prophesied that I would secure the loan I least expected from the bank. I asked for his address; he said he is yet to secure an accommodation of his own. When we were about to part, I wondered if I could get him on the phone. After a well-stretched pause, he decided to write his name and a contact number on this piece of paper."

Tracy curiously responded: "Dad, can I see the piece of paper?"

He stretched it forward, but it accidentally dropped and was blown under the big cabinet by the breeze from the oscillating fan. This was very upsetting to both Tracy and her Dad. After some fruitless efforts, it was concluded that they would both meet the man on Sunday. As her father was about to leave the office, Tracy sarcastically said! "Dad, if your in-law shows up on Sunday, which restaurant shall we go?"

Her Dad felt very cold, but responded, "You decide."

She opened the door and saw him off. The opening of the door reduced the air pressure in the room and thus the little piece of paper they had earlier on searched for was blown out from where it was before Tracy returned. With every curiosity, she picked it up. She was shocked when she saw the name Jimmy Davise and her (Tracy's) office phone number. She quickly alerted the reception on the ground floor to ask her Dad to wait for her. The disappointed man was more upset when the receptionist said he should not go yet. She spoke to him at the reception through the intercom appealing that he should please come back up to her office. Her father was very reluctant. She then said; "Dad, I know you do not mean to kill me, please come before I die." He did not catch the joke in the phrase, "Before I die" He took it as a solemn statement. He quickly agreed to return to her office. Coming to the door, he was again greeted with tears. The old man also burst into tears, his was of frustration but Tracy's of elation and high hope of God working a miracle in her life. This time around, she wiped the tears off the face of her Dad. She knelt before him and tendered her unreserved apology for being sarcastic. Her father was amazed; he couldn't understand what could have changed the whole trend within those few minutes. She narrated her dream and the telephone conversation she had and that the same person could only be the assumed angel. It was difficult for her father to believe.

There was no way they could contact Jimmy. This still kept Mr. Jackson (Tracy's Dad) in suspense till the Sunday appointment. He believed that the angel must have given that name and more so his daughter's phone number. She looked into her Dad's face as she recited Jeremiah 29:11 "For1 know the thoughts and plans that I have for you, says the Lord, thoughts, and plans for welfare and peace and not for evil, to give you hope in your outcome."

After a profound sigh, she turned to her Dad and said: "I hope what we perceive becomes a reality." He responded by opening the Bible to Jeremiah 32:27. He pointed his finger to the marked verse; " Behold, I am the Lord, the God of all flesh: is there anything too hard for me?" Tracy determined to be calm, but anxiety seemed to be written conspicuously on her forehead. There was a moment of silence after which her father said: "If this man (referring to Bro Jimmy Davise) is the same per- son; it will not be proper for us to have dinner with him on Sunday." Tracy exuberantly cut in, "Daaaad! What's wrong in my having dinner with Bro. Jimmy?"

"His status has changed," he responded. He continued, "For now it will not be proper. It will suggest my selling you cheap to him. If he is God's perfect will for your life, God will reveal to him also. She looked worried; her face expressed her doubt on the issue of God talking to Jimmy to marry her. She held her father's shoulder and whispered into his ear, "Dad, how will I know when and if God speaks to Bro Jimmy?"

"My "T" (This being the very passionate way he addresses her) he exclaimed, "Don't you have a guideline for proper courtship in your church?" Tracy realized the difference between being a teacher and the taught. She had taught these principles as a Sunday school superintendent, but strangely enough, passion seemed to have overridden reason in her mind. She came to appreciate the trauma of someone who needed help as different from the enthusiasm of the counselor at counseling. There was somebody at the door; it was one of the junior workers who wanted to collect some files which Tracy was supposed to have worked on. Her father said, "I think I have to go."

It was obvious that there had been lapses on Tracy's job during her father's long visit. She apologized to the junior officer with a promise that everything will be ready within the next hour. Checking through the files, there was not much to do. She finished the jobs and took the file to the junior officer herself. Her simplicity and apology was a challenge to the unbelieving officer. He determined to give his life to "this Jesus of my boss." His first line of action was to surprise his boss by appearing in "that their church" on Sunday. Every previous effort to make him attend the church had proved unsuccessful. Maurice who subconsciously had been excited by his decision to give his life to Christ decided to do something unusual. Coming to say good-bye to Tracy at the close of the day's job on Friday evening was a great surprise. Good Friday was supposed to be a public holiday but not at Tracy's office. It was a busy day. To Tracy, any knock at the door should be Jimmy, but this time it was Maurice. "Do you need anything?" She enquired.

"No, I just wanted to say happy Easter in advance," said Maurice.

"Thank you, but it's unlike you, what is going on?" She asked.

Maurice was not going to discuss his new-found love for Jesus. He was very sure that Tracy was going to talk as usual on the salvation of his soul. He knew that his decision was going to be the talk of the whole establishment in the next few days. He had once been suspended for being drunk during office hours. He politely shut the door and with a smile said: "Jesus is Lord." Tracy did not read any serious meaning to it but sarcasm.

The Easter Sunday service was a full house meeting because many ceremonial church members who had been absent for various reasons in the recent past were all present. It was a good problem of where to seat everybody. The ushers had a hectic day. The Sunday school was best attended in the history of the church. It almost made the most exceptional skeptic believe Jesus was coming back that Sunday afternoon. When the altar call was made; a large number of people came forward including Maurice. At the end of the service, Maurice spotted his boss at work. He felt the hour of surprise had come. He went to her to show his face. Tracy spontaneously embraced him with the statement, "Thank you for coming." His response was, "I have not just come on the invitation, but I am already in.", He turned to Mr. Jackson (Tracy's Dad) and said: "Sir it's nice meeting you again when last we met, it was a very brief moment." Mr. Jackson with an expression of surprise on his face and doubt in his voice stammered a little before he asked: "Where and when?" Maurice had to explain himself politely. As if he were to pacify the old man, he said: "I met with you at the reception door of City Actuarial Centre. I also met you at my boss' office, (pointing to Tracy) just before closing on Thursday."

Obviously, there was a mix-up in Mr. Jackson's mind. He was looking out for "the Angel." He quickly embraced the young man with a smile and tendered an apology for sounding unusually hostile during the exchange of greetings. He jokingly concluded: "I took you for an angel. Everybody laughed. However, the statement: "I took you for an angel" meant something else to a newborn babe in Christ, like Maurice. He believed the glory of God was very obvious upon him so much that he was mistaken for an angel. In his heart, he pledged to get more committed to Christ so that "the glory" may remain forever.

He turned to Tracy: "Mam, please congratulate me. I have given my life to Jesus." This information made her day. She jumped at him with an embrace, shouting: "Thank you, Jesus," three times.

Her shout called the attention of everybody around. Maurice explained how Tracy's commitment at work and especially her life and simplicity had convicted him of sin. He said he could not get over her apology of the previous Thursday afternoon and that it was on that note that he determined to become like her. To some of the listeners, his testimony became the second sermon for the day. Many purposed in their hearts to live for Jesus, as attested concerning Tracy. The whole event seemed to "add a feather to Mr. Jackson's hat".

Mr. Jackson gave Tracy a little pinch on her wrist when he whispered: "How do we get Bro Jimmy?" It was decided that they should ask of him at the Pastor's office. More so, it will be proper to introduce her father to the Pastor. The Pastor was pleased to meet Tracy and her Dad. In the course of his talk, he turned to Tracy and said: "I am sure you discussed with Bro Jimmy." "Yes sir," she responded. The Pastor went on: "Incidentally he had to return to his old station yesterday at the request of his Pastor. I guess it was to resolve or probably to dissolve his courtship with Sis. Jassy. This is an embarrassing thing to the whole church especially for the position of Bro. Jimmy as a zonal coordinator of Sunday school. I guess this is an open secret. It is a lesson to all youths to know how to possess their vessels in the Lord. Please make sure you teach again, those lessons on how to have a proper conviction and courtship as soon as the present series is over."

There was no interruption of the Pastor's speech. He spoke as if he was giving answers to the questions he would have been asked. As they were about to depart, Tracy's Dad gave an envelope to the Pastor as a token of appreciation. The Pastor held the envelope and prayed: "Lord God, I pray you to grant your son an open door, divine favor, and successes in Jesus' Name." A deep" Amen" in unison rent the room. At the entrance of the office, Tracy turned to her Pastor and said: "Sir, please on getting home remembers to remove the frozen turkey and stuff from the trunk of the car."

"When did they get there?" He questioned. Tracy said: "Manna still falls these days." They all laughed.

On their way home Mr. Jackson turned to his daughter and said: "I am getting to think that it was Bro. Jimmy that I met. I think I no more want to charge any angel for impersonation. Please let me know the outcome as soon as you get in con-tact with this "Angelic Jimmy." His puzzle and curiosity were evident. He paused, and continued: "My "T" come to think of it, we did not ask the Pastor any question! These (in reference to the development) look too real to be true." Tracy quickly cut in: "Dad, please say it is real and true." He quickly said: "It is real and true." They both laughed.

Just shortly after he secured the much desired loan from the Bank, Mr. Jackson boarded the plane the following morning to return to his home country. The loan agreement was a big surprise as he felt he was not able to meet all the requirements. This again made him think more about the "angelic personality" that prophesied the release. He returned to his home without any doubt that he had met with an angel. Deep down in his heart he desired that it should not be an angel but the real Jimmy Davise that would become his in-law if eventually, the wedding came through. With the short meaningful and loaded speech of Pastor King, he was sure that Tracy would take the proper steps on the issue of conviction and commencement of courtship.

==========================

"Manna still falls these days"

==========================

CHAPTER FIVE

PROPER COURTSHIP

Jimmy was distraught, devastated and confused by the eventual dissolution of his fifteen months courtship with Jassy. He blamed himself for many reasons. He questioned: "How did I get into this mess?" He was so depressed that he could not pray. He felt he needed help. A verse of the scripture that came into his mind was Prov. 27:17: "Iron sharpens iron: so a man sharpens the countenance of his friend (to show rage or worthy purpose)." His spirit could not agree on sharing his spiritual depression with just anybody. Being guided by the Holy Spirit, he decided to give Tracy a call. He picked up the handset, looking at the clock on the wall, it was 1.30 a.m. He did not dare to call a lady's house at such a very odd time. He dropped the handset, but he was restless and couldn't sleep. At about a few minutes to 2.00 a.m. he couldn't resist the urge to call Tracy's house any longer. His best bet was that he would drop the handset at its third ring. He thought to himself: "When did I become a menace?" "Where did I miss it? When exactly ...?" He dropped the handset again. Tears laced his eyes. He trusted that Jesus was with him, but he needed to talk to someone. He tried to call the Pastor but never had the release. After some struggle, he called the Pastor's place; the line was engaged. The Pastor was busy trying to make an international call to another part of the world, which had eight hours' time difference from Dakkoma City. He dropped the handset and chose to call Tracy in a very desperate move to avoid emotional break- down. The phone rang just twice. Tracy quickly picked it. Her best guess was that the call was international, probably from her father, though it was a terrible interruption of her emergency prayer session.

She was woken up from a horrifying dream. In the dream, Jimmy was struggling to enter into a car in an attempt to set out on a journey but was refused by the driver. He pleaded with tears to no avail. The car roared off only to burst into flames a few kilometers/miles away. She found herself and Jimmy; she never understood the mode by which they got to the scene of the accident; trying to rescue the victims. One of them was Jassy who died on the spot. Realizing it was a dream, she jumped out of bed and went straight on her knees praying. She was just about rounding off the prayer when the phone rang. She initially wanted the answering machine to pick it but was refused by the Spirit. Answering the call, she said the conventional: "Hello, God bless you." The response was a baritone voice that said: "Praise God, Sis. Tracy, I am very sorry to disturb your sleep." Recognizing the voice, Tracy screamed; "Bro. Jimmy!! Praise God." She had a caution in her spirit not to lead the talking, especially because it was Jimmy that called. After a few seconds, Jimmy said: "Do you have some minutes?'Aaaall," she responded. Her response gave him a big relief. He felt accepted at a most terrible moment of his life, more so at a very odd hour of the day. It seemed the comfort of the reception alone had solved his problem. He requested to discuss the purpose of his call when it was daytime. Tracy, however, was eager to tell him the dream. She questioned whether Jimmy could spare some minutes. "Your question is very amazing," replied Jimmy:

"If you claim to have all the time for me I guess I have all my life to listen to you at this crucial hour." This answer was beyond the comprehension of both of them. It was, however, more meaningful to Tracy. She went on to narrate her dream. She concluded that she was rounding off her prayers for him when his call came. Jimmy was silent; he struggled to hold back tears. Suddenly he burst into tears. It was the biggest shock Tracy ever received over the phone. She did not know how to handle it. She couldn't imagine the reality of grief in the life of Jimmy. She tried her best to soothe and comfort him with Scripture. She felt intimidated by his spiritual caliber and knowledge of the Scriptures. She, however, summoned up enough courage to quote "For I consider that the sufferings of this present time (this present life) are not worth being com-pared with the glory that is about to be revealed to us and in us and conferred on us!" Romans 8:18. She went further; "Many evils confront the (consistently) righteous, but the Lord delivers him out of them all. He keeps all his bones; not one of them is broken" Psalm 34: 19-20. With a tincture of smile evident in her voice she ended her recitation with; "For His anger is but for a moment, but His favor is for a lifetime or in His favor is in life. Weeping may endure for a night, but joy comes the morning". Psalm 30: 5. She added a very encouraging statement: Bro Jimmy, it is almost morning, your smiles are around the corner" There was a very deep sigh from the other end. Tracy mused with her mouth wide-opened, and her brows pushed up. She was surprised. Then came a deep emotional response: "You brought me joy this morning." Tracy's reply was: "I pray I could always."

They were both silent for a few seconds. Tracy went on: "Bro. Jimmy, why did you call?" The reply came: "You said it all." Jimmy gradually fell asleep. It was not difficult for Tracy to realize this as his speech was becoming slurred. "I guess he has slept off," she asserted. She praised God for His revelation unto her and more so the opportunity of being used to comfort a child of God. She laid back on her bed and had a profound refreshing sleep.

She woke up with some feeling of guilt. She thought in her mind as she gazed at the ceiling: 'Was I trying to sell myself cheap to Bro. Jimmy? Was I trying to win him? Did I mention anything about marriage?' These and many more questions invaded her mind. She could hardly forgive herself for the statement "I pray I could al- ways." She remembered Jimmy's statement; "I guess I have all my life to listen to you ..." Conclusively she said: "All these statements are coded; my prayer is that the perfect will of God for our lives should come to pass. She had a snappy morning prayer and set out for her office.

Since the salvation of Maurice's soul, the office had become a more exciting place for Tracy. Maurice being much younger in age and job experience gave Tracy a comfortable environment, especially when they share the Scripture during their lunch-break. On one of those beautiful moments of Bible study Maurice timidly said, "May I share with you an interesting dream I had?" To play safe, he quickly added: "You know dreams can always be hilarious. "They both laughed. He then went on to say, "It happened that you wedded Bro. Jimmy and I was there as a very small boy-ring-bearer. I woke up and laughed because I guess it must have happened many years ago when I was that young." To Tracy, the dream was not funny, but she was not going to show her interest. She jokingly said: "You must have been a wonderful dreamer when you were that young (trying to demonstrate the height of a toddler)." Zealous Maurice interrupted: "Mam, on a more serious note I was well-gifted in dreams when I was very young but as I grew up everything seemed to fade away until recently after I gave my life to Jesus. That makes me believe you may need to pray over this funny dream." Tracy had a powerful burning desire in her heart that the dream should come true but wouldn't want her conviction for Jimmy known to Maurice. Lest she discouraged him, she said: "Bro. Maurice, I believe God may be trying to assure you of the restoration of those spiritual gifts you lost when you went into the world. He may want to fulfill Joel 2:25

"And I will restore or replace for you the years that the locust has eaten - the hopping locust, the stripping locust, and the crawling locust, My great army which I sent among you in your life." They had a short prayer, and the break was over.

Ruminating over her conviction to accept Jimmy as her life partner, Tracy decided to prayerfully take every necessary step to keep her Pastor in the know of her conviction. She was timid to talk to the Pastor but prayed that God should lead Jimmy to have the same conviction about her. She prayed with this verse of the scripture: Prov. 21:1: "The King's heart is in the hand of the Lord, as are the water-courses; He turns it whichever way He wills." She conclusively said: "O Lord if it is your perfect will that Bro. Jimmy should be my husband that will make me get to heaven; please turn his soul towards me and grant me favor in his heart." She reminded God of His promise (as she believed He did) that she will be married before her 33rd birthday.

Jimmy could not understand why he suddenly developed a marital interest in Tracy. He was terrified by his experience with Jassy in the last few weeks. To him talking again to a sister for marriage would be the least on his mind. He could not call his feelings a clear-cut conviction. His mind was still perplexed; it was tough for him to discern between the prompting of the Holy Spirit and emotional infatuation. He could not forget his questionable pronouncement made while talking to Tracy over the phone two weeks ago. Neither could he dismiss Tracy's response as meaningless, but these were not enough facts to establish a conviction for marriage. A little card caught his attention at his table. He reached for it and turned it over. On it was written, "He that asketh receiveth." He was not sure whether to ask for anything. He replaced the card. He squinted to read a small imprint at the bottom of the card. It read: "...be it unto you according to your faith." He remembered Mark 11:24: "For this reason I am telling you, whatever you ask for in prayer, believe (trust and be confident) that it is granted to you, and you will (get it)." Not really in any prayer format, he said: "God give me my wife, yes my wife." There was a little knock on the door. It was an old lady from the church. He said to himself "surely this is not my wife." After exchanging some greetings, the old lady said, "Bro. Jimmy, sorry if my unscheduled visit is an intrusion on your privacy. "Not at all," he replied. The old lady went on;

"I was praying a few days ago when I had the prompting to pray for you. I did the praying, and in a clear vision, I saw you wed Sis. Tracy. I decided to ignore it. But today I was passing by; I want to believe it was the Holy Spirit that bid me call at your door, I least expected you to be at home." The old lady's visit was an answer to his simple prayers. He promised the old lady that he would pray about the subject. As she departed, he said: "She is not my wife. I guess she is her "John the Baptist. With a smile on his face, he sank to his knees. After his reasonably long prayer session, he decided to talk to the Pastor about the issue to sample his (Pastor's) opinion. He booked an appointment to see the Pastor. The Pastor's secretary gave him the next available time, not questioning the purpose of the meeting. When the Pastor checked the list of appointments for the day, he was delighted that Jimmy would be the very first person. He (the Pastor) was already going to send for him on what he called a very urgent matter.

As soon as Jimmy entered into the Pastor's office, he was offered a seat. On the floor under the chair was a picture face down. It must have fallen off the picture album the photographer came to show the Pastor. Incidentally, the photographer was not booked for an appointment. He gained the privilege because he walked straight into the Pastor, as he was about to enter the general office. The Pastor was anxious to see the pictures; therefore, he invited him (the photographer) in. The picture photograph on the floor was taken at one of the recent functions in the church. It showed the Pastor sharing some points with the Sunday School Superintendents. The key figures in the picture were Jimmy and Tracy. He looked at the image for a few seconds and handed it over to the Pastor who questioned how he came about it. He said: I found it
on the floor here in the office." The Pastor nodded his head. The action and the look on the face of the Pastor seemed to have told Jimmy everything he needed to hear.

To commence the session, the Pastor prayed a concise prayer to which Jimmy said: "Amen." "Bro, what can I do for you today?" Jimmy was not sure of how to open the chapter. He was silent for a while, then said: "Sir let's talk about the picture."? "Which picture?" the Pastor questioned. "The one I just handed over to you sir. "What about it?" said the Pastor. Jimmy was silent, but the expression on his face said it all. His actions confirmed the revelation the Pastor had and for which he was going to invite him (Jimmy) in the first place. He then said to him; "I do not have to speak for you. Let me ask you this question: Do you have any marital conviction for Sis. Tracy?" There was no audible reply, but Jimmy was close to tears, and all he could do was nod his head. The Pastor smiled. The Pastor's smile gave him a level of confidence to open up. He went on to say: "Sir, you know what I had just passed through in the last three months? To say I was confused about what having a conviction for a marriage partner is would be an aberration. The news of Sis. Tracy's wedding last month aggravated my traumatic experience."

"I guess you mean Jassy," the Pastor corrected. "O yes, I mean Jassy," he acknowledged. Staring at the Pastor, he said, "Sir it means Sis. Jassy was courting two of us simultaneously. I do not find it easy to believe she would do such a thing and still be actively involved in the services of the Lord."

The Pastor, looking very serious asserted: "Her surreptitious act is a confirmation of Job 1:6:
"Now there was a day when the sons (the angels) of God came to present themselves before the Lord, and Satan (the adversary and accuser) also came among them.'
"Sir, to the point that she got virtually involved in almost every aspect of the church?" Jimmy questioned. "But her exit from your life and the church is a proof that God answers prayers," the Pastor reiterated. Jimmy sighed "...Praise God."

"Now let's talk about your plan for marriage," the Pastor resumed.

Jimmy adjusted his sitting posture and held the seat of the chair as he tilted forward, one could almost suspect that the chair was going to give way. He unequivocally said: "Women! Women!! Women are dangerous; I am scared of them. Who on earth would have thought Sis Jassy was not a committed Christian?" With a little repudiation, he said: "I have many reasons to think or probably believe that Tracy would be my best bet for marriage, but..,." he sighed. His reasons were almost obvious. His academic, secular and material attainments were quite lower than Tracy's. It was almost possible to read his mind on his face. The Pastor ignored his repugnance of confidence and asked him whether he ever had a strong feeling for

Tracy. The Pastor could not hold back laughter when Jimmy said: "Exactly the reason why I decided to see you before I 'die.'"

The Pastor promised him that he would sample the opinion or conviction of Tracy on the issue. The promise· was of a significant relief to a "near-fainting" Jimmy who sweated throughout the discussion. His sweat in the fully air-conditioned office was of concern to the Pastor. He decided to advise him not to see the issue as a sink or swim but that "the will of the Lord should be done."

Jimmy, trying to brave the situation said: "I have committed everything to the hands of the Lord, I guess I am sweating because I am not very sure Sis. Tracy will be ready to accept me for a husband. However, if she does, I will forever love her. "The Pastor laughed as he said sarcastically: "You have truly committed everything to the hands of the Lord."

It was at this juncture that he realized his contradictions. He admittedly said:

"Sir, this experience makes me appreciate the plight of many young would-be married people in crisis moments."

The Pastor responded with these verses of the Scripture: "For we do not have a High Priest Who is unable to understand and sympathize and have a shared feeling with our weakness and infirmities and liability to the assaults of temptations but One

Who has been tempted in every respect as we are, yet without sinning." Heb. 4:15: He went further to read I Cor. I0:13: "For no temptation (no trial regarded as enticing to sin), [no matter how it comes or where it leads] has overtaken you and laid hold on you that is not common to man [that is, no temptation or trial has come to you that is beyond human resistance, and that is not adjusted and adapted, and be-longing to human experience, and such as man can bear. But God is faithful [to His Word and to His compassionate nature], and He [can be trusted} not to let you be tempted and tried and assayed beyond your ability and strength of resistance and power to endure, but provide the way out (the means of escape to a landing place), that you may be capable and strong and powerful to bear up under it patiently." Conclusively he said: "Bro. Jimmy, you need to be courageous; you cannot afford to faint. Remember Prov. 24:10: "If you faint in the day of adversity, your, strength is small." Be a man." He then prayed with him.

After some good sessions and days of prayer on Jimmy's conviction, the Pastor was convinced actually to question Tracy on the issue. The discussion was not long. It seemed the invitation by the Pastor had long been awaited. She expressed herself freely to the Pastor. The Pastor, however, did not disclose the "Jelly state' 'of Jimmy. He only promised her that he would arrange to meet with them both as soon as he feels right to do so. With a tinted smile, she responded: "Sir, not too long." A statement to which the Pastor exclaimed: "And not too soon."

This he said to assess the urgency of her desire. Her smile was a little enigmatic when she said: "Sir, my daddy has said to me: "My prayer is that you get married before I die. I am happy you met him some months ago." "Yes," the Pastor interjected. "He was full of life. He still has many more years to go." "Amen," she responded with a plea for mercy. The Pastor laughed and then prayed with her. He was personally happy and convinced that his dream would surely come to pass. In his opinion, the wedding would strengthen the church.

Not quite five minutes after Tracy's departure, Jimmy walked into the general office to sort out something concerning the programme for a youth meeting. The Pastor heard his unmistakable voice. He was prompted to settle the issue quickly. He felt the Lord wanted to give Tracy's request a definite answer. He asked his secretary to check whether she had not driven off quickly. The secretary sped to the car park and found her engaged in discussion with Associate Pastor Dickson at the gate. She shouted: "Sis. Tracy, please do not go yet; the Pastor wants you back in the office." Tracy had to cut short her discussion with Dickson and promised to give him a call later in the day.

The Pastor had invited Jimmy into his office before Tracy's return. The secretary bid her enter straight into the Pastor's office. The proposed courtship had been the desire of many members of the church. Tracy was shocked to meet Jimmy in the Pastor's office. She became shy and agitated. Her eyes dropped. The Pastor offered her a seat before he (the Pastor) left his usual position to join the two in a mini-conference setting. The meeting was brief. They both took an oath of holiness before the Pastor. It was time to go; Jimmy felt like "walking tall" as he entered into the general office only to be stunned by very curious eyes. He was surprised that Tracy did not come through the general office. She had requested the Pastor to let her out through the side door. This action confounded many of the hopeful waiting eyes. It was the beginning of a very successful courtship.

Tracy, overwhelmed with joy could not rest until she had shared the development with her father across the Atlantic. She gave him a very fulfilling phone call. It was dreams come true. Her father joyously said, "My daughter will marry my angel."

After a few minutes of discussion, Tracy sensed a beep on the line. She asked her father to stay online while she checked on the caller. It was

Associate Pastor Dickson. She eventually excused her father. It was the beginning of inconceivable telephone adultery.

CHAPTER SIX

TELEPHONE ADULTERY

Hello Pastor Dickson, how are you doing? It's been a while. Her excitement and exuberance were evident in her voice. She was heavily basking in the joy of finding true love. She realized that the devil had tried to deceive her with the impression that holy living was obsolete and opium to a good relationship. To her, the tactical insinuation of sexual fulfillment with Dickson had been overcome by God's divine intervention. She ceased to seek the "surgery" but platonic companionship. She knew quite well that her insinuations were understood by the associate pastor but believed that he should be spiritual enough to overcome it. Meanwhile, Dickson had spent the past few weeks struggling with sexual infatuation instigated by her lustful insinuations. His phone call was a ploy to get Tracy back on track towards her initially desired "surgery." He had missed his wife. This fact was obvious to Tracy. He believed that a relationship with her would be the safest. Tracy could not hold back the information of her new-found love for Jimmy. The news was not too good to Associate Pastor

Dickson. He tried to gloss over it as he sweet-talked her into their one-time discussion on "the cup of tea."

A discussion on the issue of the "cup of tea" was like a magic wand, Tracy felt some warmth. She enjoyed the discussion. It was very sexually gratifying. At one moment she confessed her desire over the "cup of tea" but quickly added, "I praise God for His faithfulness and deliverance especially for the coming of Bro. Jimmy into my life today." This was very offensive to Dickson, who had already been "burning." However, he couldn't register his disappointment. Tracy rubbed salt into his raw wound when she added: "You have always been there to relieve my passion. I hope I have assuaged the absence of Sis. Chimmy (Dickson's wife who was many miles away)." Dickson replied with a sighing voice that expressed his "fall." Tracy is a very clever and intelligent person who perceived that the purpose of the call was beyond a platonic desire. To play safe, she said jokingly, "I will invite Sis. Chimmy for a weekend visit." She laughed. Dickson also laughed but added, "You don't have to. The Lord is in control." They bid each other good-night without a word of prayer.

Dickson felt used and infatuated. Keeping his mind away from Tracy became his biggest battle. The devil deceived him to think he had missed an opportunity. He thought he could still work on

Tracy to get her over into sexual immorality. Many times he blamed himself but would still console himself that he did not start it all. He took his Bible; read over Gen. 39:9: "He is not greater in this house than I am; nor has he kept anything from me except you, for you are his wife. How then can I do this great evil and sin against God?" He also read through; Prov. 6:32-33: "But whosoever commits adultery with a woman lacks heart and under-standing moral principle and prudence; he who does it is destroying his own life. Wounds and disgrace will he get, and his reproach
will not be wiped away.

Just as he was about to close his Bible, his eyes spotted Prov. 7:21-23, "With much justifying and enticing argument she persuades him, with the allurements of her lips she leads him [to overcome his conscience and his fears] and forces him along. Suddenly he [yields and] follows her reluctantly like an ox moving to the slaughter, like one in fetters going to the correction [to be given] to a fool or like a dog enticed by food to the muzzle. Till a dart [of passion] pierces and inflames his vitals; then like a bird fluttering straight into the net [he hastens}, not knowing that it will cost him his life." He felt very insecure, used and set up; he hated himself. He burst into tears. A few minutes later he concluded to avenge himself on Tracy with all subtlety.

The telephone sexual gratification continued between them. But Tracy was determined to give her virginity as the best gift to the "husband of her youth" - incidentally, Jimmy had also never been defiled. The experience had almost driven Dickson mad. He started nursing the idea of either raping Tracy or finding solace somewhere else. He had suffered series of night- mares just a little more than Tracy, an experience they share at times when they talk on the phone. To play safe, Tracy determined not to accept any visit from Dickson and would not offer one. Their adulterous telephone discussion was no more helpful to either of them. However, Tracy felt she was at an advantage as the infatuation compelled her to speed up plans for her wedding. After one of such emotional expressions over the phone, Dickson was completely drowning in the ocean of lust. He told Tracy to drop the phone that he will call back in a few minutes. He went on WhatsApp; he switched to a video call so that he could see Tracy on his screen. Tracy was shocked to see Dickson appear only in his under pant. She was not expecting a video call. She was scantily dressed as she lied down on her couch in her sitting room. She quickly stayed away from the camera in an attempt to be properly dressed. Dickson realized that she was deliberately avoiding the camera so as not to show her nakedness. "Why are you avoiding the camera? I guess you admire my broad hairy chest, what is wrong in you showing your cleavage?" "My cleavage is for my husband; it is part of my virginity," she retorted. "If that is the case, you are not a virgin because I had seen it accidentally on one or two occasions when we went out together. I guess you must have dressed out on those outings to show me how attractive you could be; he affirmed. "Oh, you saw my cleavage accidentally! That was fine; accidents do occur. Now the owner has come, and the window is shot. The accident does not imply the loss of my virginity to you. I had almost engaged you in a 'surgery,' but the Lord delivered me from your 'dagger' now it is too late. The treasure is reserved for the lawful owner." "Are you sure?" He questioned. "O yes and I will make sure that no reoccurrence of an accident." "How about 'Pay per view'? She laughed as she said, "You are a big rascal, how much are you ready to pay per view? Do you remember pastor's nugget; 'One thing that can never be bought or sold at the right price is conscience. So what will you give?" "The totality of my being." "You are not serious, and I believe I am not the devil to whom you are ready to offer yourself."

Dickson realized that he had lost every respect in the sight of Tracy, but he could care less. He felt he could eventually talk her over into zenith of immorality or full blast defilement. Jokingly he said; "If you rest on this broad chest, you will suddenly fall asleep, yet you will still keep your virginity because I promise to keep my word not to go beyond your B-square." He made her see his turgidity which was evident under his almost translucent under-pant. The sight was very shocking and traumatizing to Tracy; she never saw anything that close before. She switched the phone off and was seriously convicted of sin by the Holy Spirit. She knelt, but she could not pray. Her phone rang; it was Dickson. She was not going to respond but was lured into a response by the devil. She picked the phone and said: "...you shocked me. I have never seen such a sight in my life." "It was just an expression of my excitement and my love for you. Now that you saw it, why not handle it." He reiterated. Stacy was quiet; she realized that she was in trouble, but a force and her lust kept her on. She heard a voice in her spirit-man that said; "You are lost and out of your mind if you do not retract yourself, you will be lost forever." She looked around the house as if someone was speaking from behind her. She remembered watching the movie: "LOST FOREVER." Dickson saw her as she looked bewildered, he questioned, "Did someone come in." "Yes, the Holy Spirit came in. He said I am lost and may be lost forever. I got to go." "Can I come over?" "If you try it you will be consumed by the Holy Ghost fire." Not in your house." He retorted. Well, you may spend the night in jail..." She hung the phone on him. She was overwhelmed by the condemnation of sin and fully convicted. She wept as she opened her Bible to Psalm 51; 91. She could not get over Dickson's final assertion that the Holy Spirit was not in her house. Her prayers were for the forgiveness of sins and the restoration of the power of the Holy Spirit.

Dickson felt like driving straight to Tracy's house, but he remembered her threats and that she had once said her virginity would be the best gift she would give Jimmy on their wedding day. He thought of direct masturbation, which he felt would be more gratifying than his usual almost regular "wet dreams." He considered finding a sister in the fellowship. "That may be disgraceful when known or should the sister decline," he asserted hesitantly. He concluded a "call-girl" would be the safest. That will necessitate the use of a condom to avoid infection especially AIDS, he thought. Just as he was about to stand from his chair, the Holy Spirit whispered to him in the usual still small voice, "Dickson-you -should- know -you - are bought- with a price. "That called his attention to 1 Cor. 6:15-20. He reached for his Bible: "Do you not see and know that your bodies are members (bodily parts) of Christ (the Messiah)? Am I, therefore, to take the parts of Christ and make (them) parts of a prostitute? Never! Never! Or do you not know and realize that when a man joins himself to a prostitute, he be- comes one body with her? The two, it is written, shall become one flesh. But the person who is united to the Lord becomes one spirit with Him. Shun immorality and all sexual looseness (flee from impurity in thought, word; 'or deed). Any other sin which a man commits is one outside the body, but he who commits sexual immorality sins against his own body. Do you not know that your body is the temple (the very sanctuary) of the Holy Spirit Who lives within you, whom you have received (as a Gift) from God? You are not your own. You were bought with a price (purchased with preciousness and paid for, made His own). So then, honor God and bring glory to Him in your body. "After reading those golden texts, he burst into tears. He reached for the phone, to call his wife (Chimmy) but had to leave a message because she was at work. The use of a telephone was not allowed on duty at her job. His message was expressive of his dangerous and tearful experience. Tremulously he said: "Please come urgently before I die.

He sent the same message by e-mail. The e-mail was not as disturbing as the shaky voice on the voice mail. One could easily sense the emotional tremor in his voice. Chimmy couldn't sleep throughout the night. Every attempt to get Dickson failed as he had disengaged his line and was off work to cut off from everybody. Chimmy immediately phoned Henry (her boss at work) who had been an old time friend of her husband. Henry was one of Dickson's converts. Every effort to get Dickson failed. Henry quickly agreed to grant Chimmy off duty for a week. The arrangement was made to make sure Chimmy got to Dakkoma city on the next available flight. Early morning of the following day, Chimmy was at the door. The doorbell

rang. Dickson opened the door; it was Chimmy. "Are you alright?" she screamed "No." Dickson replied. "But you don't look ill, "Chimmy retorted. "You are right," he said gently and emotionally as he embraced the love of his youth. He whispered to her ear, "I am sick of you." She was shocked. She exclaimed: "You almost killed me." "Lest I die," he interjected. "How? "She questioned. He locked the

front door behind her, pulled her on towards the bedroom as he said: "Come and see."

After his fill, he narrated his experience and struggles. However, he did not mention who exactly among the sisters in the fellowship was involved. Chimmy was curious but agreed not to probe any further, especially as she hardly knew any of the members of the large congregation.

The following Sunday service was an exceptional one for the telephone adulterers who were comforted by the presence of their respective lovers. The sermon, however, left them with a thin line of comfort. The theme was based on Prov. 28:13: "He who covers his transgressions will not prosper, but whoever confesses and forsakes his sins will obtain mercy." They were both convicted. After the service, there was a lot of liberty for mutual fellowship amongst the brethren. Tracy felt on top of the world when Dickson introduced her to Chimmy as the Sunday School superintendent and the fiancée of Bro. Jimmy (standing by in smiles). There was not the slightest reason for Chimmy to suspect her as the "attempted killer" of her husband. They had a very heated discussion. There was a sense of guilt deep down in Tracy's heart as she cuddled Chimmy before departure. She determined to confess to the Pastor her experience. Her repentance, confession, and determination to stay pure won the confidence and respect of the Pastor. Though Associate Pastor Dickson felt convicted of sin, he was not prepared to confess his fault to the Pastor. More so, he had less than five weeks to finish his program in Dakkoma City. When the Pastor invited him into his office to discuss his plans after the expiration of his service with the local "A- Z" Holiness Church, he was hinted that Tracy had reported a purported unholy alliance (telephone adultery) be-tween them both. He was not prepared to discuss the issue. His attitude disturbed the

Pastor. The discussion was finally closed with this note:

"Bro. Dickson (as he fondly called him) takes heed to yourself in this very exciting but 'high-risk' service to the Lord. A high-risk especially for those who cannot discipline their minds. Remember Apostle Paul's solution, 1Cor. 9: 24-27. "Do you not know that in a race all the runners compete, but (only one receives the prize) so run (your race) that you may lay hold (of the prize) and make it yours. Now every athlete who goes into conducts himself temperately and restricts himself in all things. They do it to win a wreath that will soon wither, but we (do it to receive a crown of eternal blessedness) that cannot wither. Therefore I do not Run uncertainly (without definite aim) I do not box like one beating the air and striking without an adversary. (But like a boxer I buffet my body (handle it roughly, discipline it by hardship) and subdue it, for fear that after proclaiming to others the Gospel and things about it, I should become unfit (not standing the test, be unapproved and rejected as a counterfeit)."

"Please do not lose sight of Job's legacy on integrity stated in Job 27:6: "My uprightness and my right standing with God I hold fast and will not let them go; my heart does not reproach me for any of my days, and it shall not reproach me as long as I live". Remember; we are expected to be an excellent example to the flock we lead in integrity and purity.

CHAPTER SEVEN

PURITY IN COURTSHIP

Shyness and religious sentiments pervaded the first few weeks of the courtship between Tracy and Jimmy. There was no intimate discussion. Tracy seemed not to miss anything as she got her solace in telephone adultery with Dickson. There was no doubt that they both desired getting married in the shortest time possible. Neither of them was prepared to open the discussion on the issue of planning their wedding; they were both victims of sentimental orthodoxy and religious sanctimony. Jimmy can best be described as an unadulterated puritan Christian. He was (if not too) careful of his choice of words and subject of discussion with his fiancée. His greatest thrills were the times they shared the Scriptures and discussed how to take the land for the Lord in prepa-ration for the second coming of Jesus Christ. It was divine intervention when the Pastor casually asked Tracy about their wedding plans. Her reply was "it should be any time from now, but we are yet to discuss it." The Pastor was a little curious.

Tracy intelligently gave a report that prompted the Pastor to arrange a counseling meeting for the two virgins. It was at this meeting that Jimmy's rigidity and religiosity were uprooted. Dickson had tutored Tracy on many issues; the only thing he had not succeeded in taking from her was her virginity.

Jimmy was a very well-comported brother. All his private visits to Tracy's residence were all well-timed. His most common time of visit was a few minutes to the time of fellowship in the church. At a point, Tracy felt he visited to get her to church and in good time. She requested for a time for them to go shopping together. She desired walking hand in hand in the moonlight. She felt a cuddle would not be a sin neither would a "holy kiss" (a peck on the cheek) lead to hell. None of these seemed to be of interest to Jimmy. He had an intense love and respect for Tracy. He would hardly visit without a gift for her.

A surprise birthday party organized for him by Tracy and friends turned out to be their first party time together. Jimmy was very shy and surprised. He felt a deep love for Tracy; his facial expression said everything but could not afford an embrace; to him, it will be unholy. Tracy got the signal and quickly seized the opportunity to express her love for a little romance. Her cuddle as she sang "Happy birthday to you...was greeted with a thunderous ovation from the crowd including the Pastor. To

Jimmy, it was a very unusual experience, the very first of its type. His response to the ovation was: "I guess this is not our wedding day." It was surprising as the crowd seemed to respond in unison: "We know ..." Everybody laughed. The greatest achievement of the party was the breaking of the ice. The experience brought more liberty into their courtship. They could now discuss some intimate issues.

Tracy at a point during the courtship felt uncertain of the masculine ability of Jimmy. She could not sense any warmth in him during their "intimate" discussions. She had never seen any bulge or evident contour below his waist. She thought to herself: "Could this be the reason why Sis. Jassy called it quits?" To her, he was a direct opposite of Dickson. Her fears were re-enacted when during one of their discussions Jimmy narrated his childhood upbringing. His final statement that he was a novice in the act of sex seemed to do more harm than good. Tracy could not hold back a much-unexpected question. She interjected:

"But does that mean you don't feel a desire for sex? Don't you have turgidity?" Jimmy's very modest answer was: "Occasionally."

"What is that supposed to mean?" questioned Tracy.

"Exactly the way I said it; occasionally," he replied with a muse.

His dismay was almost written on his face. It was evident that he clearly understood what Tracy insinuated. He felt that the discussion should be stopped or the subject changed. He was not interested in whatever could cause his imagination to run riot or instigate any lust in him. Suddenly he felt some warmth in his pant. This made him very uncomfortable, and instinctively he turned his gaze away from Tracy.

Jimmy focused his attention on a picture (of Jesus' ascension) on the wall. It was as if they were in two different worlds. After about two minutes, Tracy touched his shoulder to call his attention. She said, "I took that picture some years back," referring to her portrait placed by the side of the ascension. "Which picture?" he responded.

"I guess you admire my sweet look as perfectly captured in that portrait," replied Tracy. It was a challenging moment for Jimmy. He could not tell her that his focus was not on her portrait. He did not notice the portrait until she mentioned it. He hesitated for some seconds before he said:
"I was looking at the "ascension." I am sorry; I never noticed the portrait."

His answer was like cold water poured on a red hot iron. It deflated her spirit completely. She hated him for being very insensitive to her romantic expressions. Diverse imaginations ran through her mind. She reverted to her assumption on why Jassy called it to quit. She decided to terminate the discussion and end the visit. She tried to hide her disturbance. The turbulence in her soul was evident on her face, but she purposed in her mind not to express her feelings. She hardly realized that she was cold and not any more enthusiastic. Her voice quivered as she said: "Bro. Jimmy, you may have to go; I guess I have a lot of paperwork to do on my current project in the office."

Jimmy, who was coming back into the discussion, could hardly fathom where things went wrong. To him, his statement and · attitude did not call for such a pulsation in a reaction as expressed by Tracy. He knew something was wrong; however, he chose to respect her opinion. His , heart throbbed when Tracy turned down his request for prayers. For the very first time, he stretched forth his hand to touch Tracy's shoulder. With a tremble in his baritone voice, he said, "My 'T' (having heard her father address her so), what went wrong? The phrase "My 'T' reminded Tracy of the affectionate and passionate approach of her father. She felt it was a grave contradiction in a moment like this. She could not contain herself as she burst into tears and sank into the sofa. Jimmy almost fainted when he saw the assumed "iron lady" wobble like Jelly. He screamed: "Sis. Tracy! What is happening, and what did I do? What is going on?" He got no answer but a hooting sob, to which he responded "Oh, my God!"

He couldn't touch her, as he was not very sure that his hand, which he had earlier placed on her shoulder, did not induce the crying! A few minutes later, Tracy raised her head just to advise Jimmy to leave. She was shocked to realize that Jimmy was standing with his two hands on his head, tears rolling down his cheeks without any reservations. The sight was too much for Jimmy to handle. He said to Tracy: "I am very sorry, I am sorry, I mean I am very sorry."

He was baffled. In his imagination, he felt his close-ness and touch of Tracy's shoulder was wrong. He pleaded, "My sister, please forgive me. I am very very sorry. I think I have to go, will that be okay?" he questioned. He reached for his bag out Of which he brought out a pack of six new handkerchiefs. He gave one to Tracy to wipe her face while he placed the packet on the table. He looked at her and said, "I did not bargain for this when I bought these handkerchiefs on my way." Ironically the statement made Tracy laugh. It sounded funny to them both, and they laughed together. Jimmy's laughter was very brisk. He paused and asked again.

"On a very serious note, Sis. Tracy, what did I do wrong?"

Tracy realized that the question revealed Jimmy's innocence, she then purposed in her heart not to condemn him for his assumed insensitivity, lack of affection and passion. Her response was: "Bro. Jimmy, I appreciate your focus on Jesus, but you may have to realize that I am also now in your life. Your reply; "I was looking at the ascension, I am sorry I never noticed the portrait" made me feel very miserable, unimportant, unnoticed and probably unwanted. I know that you love Jesus; you have known him before meeting me. You need to realize that I am also now a part of your life. I felt you might never have time for me."

She stared at his face as if to affirm her assertion. She went on: "You made me weep when you tied your "insensitivity" to my father's passionate way of calling me "My 'T'"

To Jimmy, these reasons were not enough to cause such level of emotional breakdown. However, it was a storm in a teacup. He thought in himself: "this is a lesson I have to learn." He could not imagine the delicate nature of his fiancé. And probably some other women as well. He realized that a higher level of maturity was required for any one man who wanted to get married. To him, it was a task to love the Lord and a spouse. He remembered his pastor's quotable quote, "The ability to manage responsibilities with legitimate distractions without disruptions is the true proof of maturity." He questioned himself whether he actually had a clear understanding of 1John 4:20-21: "If anyone says, I love God and hates (detests, abominates) his brother (in Christ) he is a liar; for he who does not love his brother, whom he has seen, cannot love God, whom he has not seen; And this command (charge, order, injunction) we have from Him: that he who loves God shall love his brother (believer) also."

There were different thoughts going on in both their minds. The atmosphere was no longer tense; Tracy was ready to have a word of prayer. To her, the tide was over, to Jimmy it was the beginning of the storm. He was still much agitated over the "tear flow" of the night. He suddenly realized that it was almost 12.00 midnight the shock of the "sudden flight" of time was evident on his face. He stared at the wall clock for some seconds, checked on his wrist-watch for a confirmation. To him, it was almost a conspiracy in the world of watches and time. He said to Tracy: "Shall we pray?"

He was very much in a hurry, not because of a busy schedule but due to a sense of guilt. How would he explain it, if anybody got to see him corning out of a sister's house at about midnight?

He desired a very brief prayer. It was a "mistake" when he asked Tracy to pray, believing she was more eager to bring the meeting to a close. Instead of Tracy saying a word of prayer she decided to lead a session of prayers. For the first five minutes, Jimmy was engrossed in deep thought about his integrity and the probable genuineness or sincerity of Tracy's earlier request for his departure. He felt like stopping the prayers but was scared of being charged for "prayerlessness." After the first ten minutes, he agreed to flow along in the prayer session. Tracy seemed to be caught up in the spirit as she raised one prayer point after another. To her, it was a dialogue between lovers. She felt she was in the best hour of her life: talking with her two lovers - Jesus and Jimmy. At the expiration of the "maximum time"; as fixed in his mind, he became restless and was eager to stop the prayer than expecting any new prayer point. Tracy was not time conscious at all; she entered into the forty-fifth minute of the prayer session. Jimmy cleverly checked on his wrist-watch. It was half-past twelve in the night. Spontaneously he said, "In Jesus name, we've prayed." There was no response of "Amen" from Tracy. Jimmy went on to round off the prayer session. His first statement was; "Father we thank you for this night. It is beyond 12.30 a.m. We thank you because you are a God of order ..." The first few statements were obviously to Tracy rather than God. It was at this juncture that Tracy realized that it was not proper for Jimmy to be in her house at that very odd hour of the night. She said an intense Amen to every prayer made by Jimmy. Her agreement was evident in her response. Jimmy was happy to have been able to register the error in their timing. Her excitement was probably responsible for extending the round of prayer a little longer than what Jimmy expected.

They parted in very high spirit but not with even a handshake. Tracy was ready for a hug but to Jimmy, a handshake at such a time in the night could be very dangerous. It was the first time that Tracy suspected what she believed was a visible bulge below his waist. His quick tum towards the door was suggestive of the fact that, he had some-thing to hide. It was sound proof and much-desired sight for Tracy. She was reasonably convinced that Jimmy was a complete but highly disciplined and responsible person. Jimmy walked briskly to his car. He started the engine and sneaked away with the lowest noise possible. Tracy stood and watched the car drive out of sight. She returned into her sitting room, sank into the sofa with joy and a sense of fulfillment. She saw the person of Jimmy as a complete departure from of the person of Dickson. She was able to understand the true meaning of love, compared to the obsessive lust that existed between her and

Associate Pastor Dickson. Her passion for Jimmy was greatly enhanced by the experience of the night, She thought. "He wants my virginity; he will surely have it on our wedding night." She went into a session of worship to appreciate the mercies of God and His grace that delivered her from the lustful entanglement she had with Dickson. To her the night was one of the best moments of her life; it was really "sadness and joy."

Tracy was ready for a hug but to Jimmy, a handshake at such a time in the night will be dangerous.

CHAPTER EIGHT

SADNESS AND JOY

Jimmy's safe return home from a very "dangerous" but uncorrupted visit was an enjoyable success. A deep love for Tracy started bubbling in him. He could almost see her everywhere in his own home. He reached for her picture, which accompanied her birth- day gift for him. He looked at it with every passion but felt he was becoming obsessed. The thought of any further conflict or a break in courtship gripped his heart probably harder than the black- smith's vise would hold a piece of metal. He could not get over those moments of tears. He felt a repeat of such incidence might not end the same way. He became terrified of another broken courtship. He felt losing Tracy would be the end of his dream of getting married in life. He lost his sleep.

The excitement that gave him the warmth had disappeared. He got into a fix that soon grew into despair. Prayer became repulsive while Bible study was repudiated. The devil victimized him and tormented by the fear of uncertainty. It was really his "midnight" hour. For the first time, he counted the ceiling tiles in his bedroom as his eyes went to and fro the whole ceiling. He seemed to have murdered sleep. He blamed himself for every error. He retrospected and realized the probable reason why his first courtship was destroyed. He questioned again how he came into a conviction for Jassy. He compared it with the one he had for Tracy. To him, the error was not too much on his person but more on the style and approach given to the issue, more so, the unchristian lifestyle of Jassy. He recalled that after he had what he called a "God-given" conviction, he just went straight to share it with Jassy who seemed to have been waiting for his gesture. He had no counselor or anybody actually to meet for guidance when things started going wrong. He concluded that that was the major problem. He realized that there is a great difference between the two courtships. In his soliloquy, he said: "I really need help. I know Jesus will always be there, the Holy Spirit is ever ready, yet I must talk to somebody on this issue."

The Pastor was his best bet especially as he (the Pastor) was involved at the beginning of it all. He decided to seek counsel from the Pastor. The concept of remembering the involvement of the Pastor was like an overdose of tranquilizer. He suddenly fell into a deep sleep.

His sleep was just playback of his visit to Tracy. His subconscious mind actually was very overwhelmed with his passion and love for Tracy, which he was able to control at the close of the meeting. He was almost at the verge of having a wet dream when he suddenly woke up. His spirit man was obviously stronger than the lustful imagination and fantasy that pervaded his dream. It was his worst experience close to a wet dream. He gave it diverse interpretations. Looking at the clock, he realized that he had probably hardly slept for an hour. He was afraid of sleeping lest the inevitable happened. He knelt down and prayed to sanctify the whole house and to cast away every spirit of lust ... But just as he was about to round off the prayer, the devil sneaked into his subconscious mind to suggest that he was being manipulated by an evil spirit in the life of Tracy. Mistakenly he took this to be the voice of the Holy Spirit. As he was .fighting it off, the devil brought to his mind, John 10:27: " The sheep that are my own hear and are listening to My voice, and I know them, and they follow Me." The devil concluded the instigation by asking him "whose sheep are you?" This clever "knitting" by the devil swept him off balance. He now had yet another "good reason" why the Pastor must be consulted. He got so confused that he could neither sleep nor pray. Time, this time around, "refused to move." He looked at the clock; it was as if he was watching a slow-motion movie. Suddenly, the Holy Spirit whispered to his soul to cast his mind back on the testimony of the life of Tracy ... On this note, he fell asleep. The Holy Spirit continued to work on him in his subconscious mind. He had a wonderful dream about heaven. He actually saw Tracy at the celebration of saints in heaven. When it was daybreak, however, he was still confused. The Scripture "I know my sheep ..." kept coming back to his spirit.

He determined to meet with the Pastor. He was very sure of the opportunity and privileges he enjoyed any time he chose to see the Pastor. He never had to go through the bureaucracy and protocol. The devil invaded his mind very slowly telling him not to be afraid of another broken courtship as: "a broken courtship is better than a broken marriage." He was prepared to challenge the Pastor should he try to encourage him to go ahead in the relationship with Tracy. The devil had said to his mind: "Don't you realize that the Pastor has a special interest in you marrying Tracy?"

As usual, Jimmy was well-received by the receptionist. He was granted automatic access to the Pastor's secretary whose broad smile was more than welcoming. He was granted permission to see the Pastor and fortunately, it was one of the Pastor's less busy days.

It was not too difficult for the Pastor to discern the fact that Jimmy's mind had been terribly poisoned by the devil, as he narrated every reason why he could no longer get along with Tracy. He drew the curtain on the discussion by saying, "I heard the voice after my prayers on the issue."

The Pastor was very agitated but did not show it. He did not make any statement in approval or disapproval of any of the points raised by Jimmy. This attitude of the Pastor actually disarmed the devil that had already prepared Jimmy for the opposition.

The Pastor meditated in his spirit and was entirely guided by the Holy Spirit on what to say. He interrupted Jimmy's statement "a broken courtship is better than a broken ..."

"Sorry to interrupt you," the Pastor apologized: "I guess you have had your conclusions before coming into this office. May I just let you know that I have nothing to lose if you miss God's choice for your life. Though it may give me pain if you do not accomplish the purpose of your calling in the ministry, let it be known that as a "father in the Lord," I have prayed for your success. My interest in both of you is that you succeed in the ministry and get to heaven at the end of it all."

The mention of heaven seemed to unveil and illuminate Jimmy's mind. It was evident on his face, but he heard a voice:

"Don't be deceived."

He probably was not aware or in control of his mind when he re-echoed through his mouth what the devil whispered to his mind. He said: "Sir, I will not be deceived."

There was silence; it was apparent that the Pastor was crossed. He stared into his eyes as if to probe his mind. Jimmy felt very sorry and sincerely apologized. His apology was however not satisfactory enough as he concluded: "I want to believe it is over." The phrase was a difficult one for the Pastor to comprehend He was left to discern exactly what was over with. Was it the courtship or the offensive statement? However, he chose not to probe the issue any further. Jimmy looked very sober and worried, but the Pastor wore a straight face. He (Jimmy) felt lonely and deserted by all. It was difficult for him to express his feelings to the Pastor whom he had just offended. He had not the courage to think of talking to Tracy. There was silence in the room. Suddenly he burst into tears and sobbed. The Pastor chose to be indifferent. He sobbed expecting the Pastor to come to his rescue. The Pastor himself could not understand why he was motionless. It was the Holy Spirit's way of dealing with Jimmy. The Pastor's "indifference" gave him the impression that the whole world was against him and that he no longer had the spiritual support of the Pastor. He felt life was not worth living. He wished the Lord should come that moment to 'take him home.' He was lost in thought. He did not realize that the Pastor had stood up from his seat. He decided to raise his head in an attempt to storm out of the Pastor's office when he realized that the Pastor was standing over him and ready to lift him up. His sudden discovery sparked another run of tears down his already "flooded" face. He experienced the warmth and the heart of a father.

The Pastor pulled him up from the chair, embraced him and said: "May the peace of the Lord rule over your spirit, soul, and body." He responded with a seraphic Amen. He was no longer ready to go, but the Pastor had little or no more time for him. The Pastor's last statement was: "Bro. Jimmy, as you said, all may be over. However, I will advise that you do not communicate it to Sis. Tracy. When you are very sure of your stand, let me know. It will be proper for you to end it all in a peaceable way so that the devil does not destroy your lives. I wish you happy days ahead. God bless you."

Jimmy left the Pastor's office convinced of his love for Tracy but confused by the voice of the devil. That day was one of the saddest days of his life. He had nobody to relate with. He could not indict his Pastor for anything. He, therefore, came again under self-condemnation. It was a miserable time for him.

Tracy, being a career lady had been very busy with her job. It never occurred to her to give Jimmy a call after her last two messages left on his answering machine (voice mail) were not given any reply. She never attributed it to any disagreement, more so as their last meeting ended with a good session of prayers.

It was Wednesday night. Tracy was unable to attend the mid-week programme due to the pressure of her job. She had earlier left a message for the Pastor through his secretary and his wife at home respectively. The Pastor did not find the message clear or convincing enough especially as Jimmy was successfully deceived by the devil not to attend the service so as to avoid contact with Tracy. The Pastor had not shared the development with anybody including his wife. In his assumption, he concluded, "Jimmy must have spoken to Tracy, and things have gone out of hand." He was reluctant to give Jimmy a call. His call to Tracy's house was picked up after the phone had rung endlessly. Tracy picked up the phone. Her rush from the door to the phone made her voice flutter a little. She did not recognize the caller's voice as the Pastor's. She said, "May I know who is speaking?"

The question shocked the Pastor, whose "hello" many times in the past had always been easily identified by Tracy. He felt something must have been going wrong. He said, "I guess if you no longer recognize my voice, I had better get off the phone...._"

It was on this note that Tracy realized it was him. She had to explain how she rushed into the house to pick up the phone. To the Pastor, her explanation lacked credence. He felt he could hear the voice of a man talking in the background. Just at that point, she switched off her little "walk-man" as the battery was getting weak. In the Pastor's perception, the man in the background was cautioned not to talk any more. However, he chose to give her the benefit of the doubt. He inquired why she was absent at the mid-week service. She was shocked, assuming her messages did not get to the Pastor. Her claim to have left messages with his secretary and his wife looked a little ambiguous. The Pastor chipped in: "I was told you would be absent from the service."

"Yes sir, "she quickly responded and gave a detailed explanation.

The Pastor believed her story but was still a little worried about her fluttered voice and the cheery sound he heard in the background.

Dropping the phone, the Pastor decided to call on Jimmy, but the call was not picked. His imagination ran haywire; he dropped the phone and sank into his chair. Not quite two minutes the doorbell rang. He rose to open the door; it was Jimmy. This visit was Jimmy's best visit ever. He was more than welcome though he was not invited and he didn't notify his host of his coming. His visit dispelled the Pastor's fear. His (Pastor's) conclusions were: "At least I am now very sure that Jimmy was not in Tracy's house."

Jimmy apologized to the Pastor for his attitude when last they met and explained all his pains and troubles. These were the very reasons why he was not able to come for the mid- week service. He requested that the Pastor should pray for him. He took time to explain some of the problems in his family background. How his father, a Muslim did not marry his mother until after being jilted by three other women. He requested that the Pastor should break every generation curse off his life. Rounding off his prayer request he said, "Sir, now that Jassy had jilted me and Tracy has left me, I guess I am towing the same line with my father."

He assumed that the Pastor had communicated his Satan- inspired break in the courtship to Tracy, especially as Tracy had not given him a call since their last meeting, not realizing that the disturbance in his mind had kept him off checking his voice mail. The Pastor paused and asked him whether he had spoken to Tracy on the issue. His answer was: "Sir, we have not spoken or seen each other since I left your office." The Pastor was a little relieved. He questioned whether he still had any conviction for Tracy. A question to which he replied:

"I will be more than willing to marry her now! Now!! Now! If she is still interested in me." The Pastor prayed for Jimmy and promised to arrange an appointment for them both in his office soonest.

The maturity of the Pastor in not divulging any information paid off, as no one else knew about the confusion Jimmy went through. It was tough for

Jimmy to believe that he was the only one involved with the devil in the "one-man army war." He returned home to notice the blip on his voice mail. The messages showed the dates. Out of the six messages, four were from Tracy. The first two messages were enthusiastic and romantic; the third was of little discouragement while the fourth expressed desertion. Jimmy realized how much damage the devil had done to him. He chose to use the devil's message against him. He said, "I henceforth choose not to be deceived by the devil. He recognized how the devil successfully distorted the application of the scripture: John 10:27: "1 know my sheep, and my sheep hear my voice." He came to appreciate what Apostle Paul meant when he wrote to Timothy in 2Timothy 2:15: "Study and be eager and do your utmost to present yourself to God approved (tested by trial), a workman who has no cause to be ashamed correctly analyzing and accurately dividing (rightly handling and skillfully teaching) the World of Truth." It implies that if care is not taken, one could wrongly apply the Scripture.

He took the phone to give a belated return call to Tracy. Meanwhile, Tracy was already anxious, and the devil also invaded her mind. However, her hectic schedule with her project in the office had kept her occupied. She received Jimmy's call with the highest enthusiasm ever.   Jimmy was ashamed to share any of his experience with her. He only apologized for being unable to return her calls due to what he called negligence on his part. After the conversation, he felt on top of the world. His hope and aspiration for marriage became much higher than that of Tracy. He was anxious to hear from the Pastor. He took a copy of his diary and the church calendar to look for a probable date before meeting with the Pastor.

The issue of the wedding had been a very vital part of Tracy's prayer life in recent times. The Lord had spoken to her in her spirit, of a particular date. Incidentally, it was to be the Saturday that would precede her 33rd birthday. She was not happy with the date. She felt any disruption of that date would mean a breach of God's promise to her. She felt some earlier dates would be better. She mentioned the issue to her dad who was yet to get back to her on the possible date. She, however, informed him that the Pastor would determine the date of the wedding.

CHAPTER NINE

THE WEDDING DATE

It was a very long night for Pastor King. He did not choose to keep a vigil but was more than disturbed by the intense prayer session held in his home. The unplanned prayer meeting was birthed by the discussion and counseling session between Deaconess Betty (the Pastor's wife) and Tracy. Tracy chose to spend her weekend holiday with the Pastor's family to afford her the privilege of a good time of counseling and sharing especially with the Pastor's wife. She purposed to acquire some information and ideas on how to run a successful home. She had read many kinds of literature on Christian marriage. She found it a special privilege to have a dialogue with a Christian author on marriage. She had always viewed Deaconess Betty as a wonderful counselor, "mother" and a friend. This visit actually revealed many more wonderful qualities, ideals, and ideas which the Pastor's wife had to offer. The meeting after the family altar initially had the Pastor in attendance until the issues and subjects of discussion turned absolutely feminine. The Pastor excused himself to give them every liberty.

"Women are good at 'gisting' " the pastor asserted. They all laughed.

It was an unusual opportunity for Tracy. She chose to exploit it to the fullest. She asked as many questions as came to her mind. She wanted to know what it really means to be a married woman and especially a pastor's wife. The Pastor's wife did not shy away from any of her very intimate and inquisitive questions. "Being a married woman is enough a challenge, to cope as a pastor's wife is a great additional responsibility. Not many understand or appreciate the challenges a pastor's wife goes through. Many members of the church who could not confront the pastor on some issues vent their pains or vendetta on his wife or children. You just have to know how to comport yourself. One of the greatest temptations a pastor's wife could face is having trust or confidence in any member of the church". Looking straight into the eyes of Tracy she affirmatively said, "I do not mean to scare you; I am almost sure you may soon become a pastor's wife just be ready to receive a haul of blames and probably occasional commendation on special events." Tracy cut in; "Such as 'MOTHERS DAY CELEBRATION.' They both laughed. "One very important thing I think I need to tell you is that you do not allow anything to erode the confidence you both have in each other. You may come to realize that some female brethren may just desire to be around your husband. If you do not trust him well enough, it may have an adverse effect on your relationship. Yes, you need to have confidence in your spouse, but that does not mean you do not register your displeasures especially any lady that you do not feel comfortable with amongst those who chose to get close to your husband. You need a lot of wisdom to communicate your displeasures." "I guess I will not want Bro. Jimmy to become a pastor. He is good enough as a Sunday school superintendent." "But you cannot limit him in his service to God." The pastor's wife cautioned. "Nooo, I promise not to hinder him in any of his desires to serve and please God. I cannot forget pastor's sermon on the 'living sacrifice.' It is only challenging if and when you, what or whom you love so dearly is the sacrifice or to be offered." "Yes, I know that may not be funny." Deaconess Betty responded. She proved to have nothing to hide.

It was one of the best nights in the life of Tracy. Deaconess Betty was quite aware of her husband's diary and appointments. She realized that he had just accepted an invitation to minister at a non-denominational city-wide crusade meeting slated for the very Saturday proposed by Tracy as a prospective date for her wedding. She expressed this clash on the date and event. The news was of great disturbance to Tracy who had anticipated a negative development concerning that date. She could not hold back her emotion. She was tearful. Deaconess Betty had not the least intimation of what could have prompted the tears. She was very empathetic; she went round to her to comfort her and actually get her to express the cause of "hot-tears." With a little hooting as she sobbed, she stammering muttered some words:

"I - anticipated this, I knew the devil would make my 33rd birthday a sad day. I... I... I am... chd ... Hooohooo." Deaconess Betty thought the matter was more serious than the issue of just moving a proposed wedding date. Her imagination was fully stretched. She thought of every possible factor that could make a young lady become very desperate about getting married in the shortest time possible. She could not fully entertain the possibility of the first thought that came to her mind, which was: "Could it be that Tracy had just defiled herself and had conceived?" She paused for a while as she stared at Tracy. She passionately asked, "My beloved sister would you tell me exactly why you are desperate to marry before or on this particular date?" Though her expression was passionate and affectionate, her use of the word "desperate" sent a clear message to the mind of Tracy. "I am not desperate, I am only apprehensive of the circumstance of my life and especially that of my father," she retorted. "Can you be a little more explicit?" urged Deaconess Betty.

"Ma, it has been my prayer that I would get married before I am 33 years old. It seems obvious that no Saturday before my 33rd birthday is available in the Pastor's diary. I cannot imagine the Pastor not present at my wedding. I would feel God did not hear my prayers on this issue. I thought I did all the prayers and fasting necessary to impress God on this matter." She, but they eventually rolled down her cheeks. "Why! Why!! Why!!!?" she exclaimed.

"Why what?" asked Deaconess Betty.

"Why should my father die before I get married?" she asked as if the Pastor's wife had her father's life in her hands.

"Who?...Who was going to kill your Dad?" questioned Deaconess Betty.

"No! No!! No!!! I cannot imagine it happen. It will spoil my life," reiterated Tracy.

"Is your father ill?" questioned Deaconess Betty.

"Yes, he was diagnosed with cancer a few weeks ago." There was silence in the room. He had always talked about my getting married. His dream is that I will give him the opportunity of seeing his grandchildren," affirmed Tracy.

"How old is he?" asked Deaconess Betty. Tracy replied: "He is over seventy years old."

"He must have married late I presume," said Deaconess Betty.

"No, my parents had a very long delay before they had me. I have spent a sizeable part of my prayer time breaking every generation curse in my life. It is my belief that I will not experience such delay in Jesus name." A prayer to which Deaconess Betty said a loud Amen. It was this sharing of pain and fears of uncertainty that actually birthed the noisy and aggressive prayer session of the night.

The fact remained that the Pastor's appoint-ment for the 30th of September had to be canceled to afford Tracy the opportunity to wed on that day. One would wonder why they had to pray so loud especially when they were aware that there were other occupants in the house. It was almost a conscious effort to wake the Pastor up (if he was already asleep). His decision was the object of their prayer. One just has to conclude that they were praying to the Pastor. Their strategy actually paid off to some extent. The aggression expressed in their prayer generated some curiosity in the Pastor. He could not hold back asking his wife, shortly, why they chose to disturb the whole house. The question was an excellent opportunity for the clever wife `to emotionally express the stress, and pain Tracy was going through. She went closer to him with an embrace, her two hands over his shoulders and a passionate look into his eyes she said "I wish Sis Tracy's desire be granted. God answers prayer. He (the Pastor) jokingly said "An answer may be yes or no" "You are His ambassador; we look up to you for His answer. Remember Tracy is your daughter," she reiterated. Her presentation was so convincing that the Pastor did not think twice before he agreed to grant Tracy the honor of having her wedding at the expense of the Pastor's newly scheduled appointment. He promised his wife that he would cancel his tentative agreement to minister at the city-wide crusade. Deaconess Betty cut in to say: "Darling, you may not have to cancel the appointment," realizing that the crusade would not start before 5.00 p.m. on the same day. "You know you do not attend wedding receptions."

"Not that of Sis. Tracy and Bro Jimmy" replied the Pastor. "Favoritism," she charged.
"No, they deserve it," the Pastor asserted.
Deaconess Betty was overjoyed by her husband's decision to honor Tracy and Jimmy specially. She was anxious to let Tracy know about the possibility of her wedding coming up just a day before her 33rd birthday. She, however, would not break the ethics and principles of ministerial commitments. She had to wait for the Pastor (her husband) to communicate the final decision to the proposed couple.

Tracy was quite aware that the Pastor was awake at the end of their prayer session because she overheard a discussion shortly before she fell asleep. When the day broke, she was a little agitated and inquisitive about the discussion between the Pastor and' his wife. She had two thoughts, either that the Pastor was really upset by their noise or that he overheard their prayers and was responsive by discussing the issue with his wife. She was very helpful to the Pastor's wife in getting through the house chores. She stylishly asked her (the Pastor's wife) a leading question on the issue of the wedding date. The experienced lady gave an ambiguous reply, which kept Tracy in suspense but not with any awkward imagination. Her ex-pressions were suggestive of good news. She just refused to break her code of ministerial conduct. She challenged Tracy with a song: "Why worry, when, you can pray, trust in Jesus and he will lead the way, don't be like the doubting Thomas, but rest on His promise, why worry, worry, worry, when you can pray?" She was very anxious to give Tracy the assurance of peace without feeling guilty of pre-empting the Pastor. It was a very wonderful experience for Tracy having to spend her weekend holiday with the Pastor's family. She enjoyed her interaction with the "Pastor's lambs" as they were called.

The Pastor had told the church that it is goats that give birth to kids while sheep give birth to lambs. It sounds unique and animating when members of the church address the Pastor's children as "Pastor's lambs" though it may sound very unfamiliar to new members of the church and especially people outside the local congregation. She realized that the children were not actually as gentle and saintly as they comported themselves when in church. She witnessed one or two occasions when they needed "Iron hand" to make them conform. She felt they were actually like every other kid and had to undergo training on becoming lambs. She learned and appreciated the level of affection between the "lambs" and their shepherd (Pastor). She sensed a deeper relationship between the children and their mother than with their father except for the baby of the family who was always clinging on to the dad. She questioned Deaconess Betty on why the grown-up children were closer to her than the Pastor. Her reply was:

"You must have realized that your Pastor is a disciplinarian both in the church and at home. He enforces structure in the home.

When I say structure, I mean everything should be done properly and in order. He expects the children above ten years old to learn conformity with law and order. These teenagers feel an encroachment on their liberty. They know that he loves them, but in most cases, he would not spare them. Though by nature, I am also strict I have to play it low so that we do not lose the children to the world of peer pressure. They see me as succor when they get it hard from their dad. We have successfully played on their intelligence in this task of PARENTING."

It was time to go to church on Sunday morning. This definitely would terminate Tracy's holiday. She called the children together to appreciate them. She commended their behavior and the domestic assistance they gave their mother. She closed her address by saying,

"... and I hope you are learning to comply with daddy's instructions? You will realize that his teachings and instructions have been helpful in making me who I am today."

She was surprised by the response of one of the children who was eleven years old.

"Aunty, we thank God for daddy; he is a good Pastor. We are his children not 'members of his congregation.' You are." They all laughed.

The laughter was just dying down when the teenager chipped in: "He is also a loving and lovable dad but just too old-fashioned and uninformed about my taste. "This comment really made them all laugh so loud that it attracted the attention of the Pastor. There was a sudden silence as they heard the sound of his voice. He asked: "What is going on." The teenagers replied, "It is daddy's appreciation day with Aunty Tracy..." They all laughed again as the Pastor responded: "Thank you for your appreciation ... you will always live to thank God and appreciate me... God bless you all."

The church service was another wonderful time in the presence of the Lord. The sermon was inspiring; the ministration was wonderful. There was no doubt that everyone in the church was touched. Tracy was still basking in the joy of her trip to the Pastor's family when she ran into Jimmy at the door on her way out. She did not actually see him until he modishly pulled her arm and asked,"... will you walk past me?"

The uniqueness of his voice brought Tracy back to the same realm with everyone around. She responded:

"Darling".

The word "Darling" was a shocker to Jimmy who was never so addressed in the six months of their courtship. Many who never knew that there was any relationship between the two had their first glimpse of the possibility of any conjugal development be-tween them. Jimmy quickly passed to her the information that the Pastor would like to meet with them on Wednesday after the special service.

'Wednesday?" questioned Tracy.

"Yes, "replied Jimmy, with a little reservation.

He wondered why Tracy was shocked about meeting with the Pastor on Wednesday. He wanted to know her state of mind. He asked,

"Will, you not attend the Wednesday meeting?"

"I will surely be around." She responded. They parted. It was a very casual discussion. Tracy was still thinking of all she learned and heard during her holiday with the Pastor's family.

She recalled the Pastor's wife's advice on her ministerial role and the support she would need to give to Jimmy:

"My beloved sister, there is no doubt that you are both prospective ministers of the gospel if Christ tarries. I have watched your progress in the past few years. I have every reason to believe you have what it takes to be ministers of the gospel. Please realize that your success begins at the place of respect for your husband. The more you respect him, the better he will be respected by others, and you will be honored and appreciated.

"May I advise you on the issue of leadership and control in the family. You will need to show more regard for him. Realize you are better read than him. If I am right, he has just the first degree while you hold a Ph.D...Presently you earn more money than he does. My sister, you need humility to keep your home. I know Bro. Jimmy to be a very maturing Christian. One would want to believe that he would not be paranoid or intimidated in any instance. However, you will play safe if you do not give any impression of control over him. This is a sensitive issue. May the Lord grant you wisdom."

"From our discussions thus far, I have come to realize how very close you are to your dad and how very much you love and respect him. May I advise that you do not compare Bro. Jimmy to your dad especially on those areas where 'he may not measure up to the level of your father's ability."

"If I heard you correctly, you said his father is an Islamic fundamentalist and that he grew up with him before giving his life to Jesus when in college. May I advise that you watch out for authoritative .control? To the best of my knowledge, Islamic fundamentalists' have strong control over their wives. If he grew up in such an environment, he would also tend to exercise some control. He may occasionally refer you to Ephesians 5:22-23: "Wives, be subject (be submissive and adapt yourselves) to your own husbands as (a service) to the Lord."

"I do not mean to say he will do this but realize that man is a product of his environment and experience. I am just saying; prepare your mind."

As she continued to remember many of the issues that were discussed, the one that gave her the most concern was the aspect of control and Islamic fundamentalism. She determined to conquer everything on her knees. She remembered her Pastor's statement: "Knee benders are stronger than iron benders. If you can bend your knees in prayers, the circumstance will be bent or broken."

To Tracy and Jimmy, the days just moved too slowly. They were very anxious to meet the Pastor on Wednesday as agreed. They had had a series of telephone conversations on the probable reason why the Pastor would want to meet with them. Tracy could guess more accurately while Jimmy suspected that it might be the after- math of Tracy's visit to the Pastor's house. He had different thoughts: "Could Tracy has complained about my insensitivity, high-handedness, lack of interest in going out together too often...?" He searched his mind. He could not think of anything that could implicate or indict him concerning their courtship. He was almost congratulating himself when he remembered the very fierce argument he had with Tracy on the issue of female circumcision.

The argument was so hot that she threatened to quit the relationship if Jimmy insisted that the yet unborn female children should be circumcised when they are born. It was their final agreement to seek the Pastor's opinion and the biblical principle on the issue. His countenance fell. Worries immediately took over his mind which became a very terrible battle ground for unimaginable satanic assault. The glass of water he was about to drink slipped off his hand and smashed into pieces on the floor. He was really confused. He determined to get himself together as he was busy doing the cleaning up of the broken glass. He sat on the chair, lost in thought. He could not imagine what the Wednesday meeting had in stock. In his guess, he suspected that this could be the probable reason why, last Sunday, Tracy was about to walk past him in the church. However, be remembered that she addressed him as darling; but that was not enough to defuse the "time bomb" that was planted in his soul by the devil.

He drifted into hallucination. He reverted into the fear of his father's experience of being jilted before marriage. Suddenly, he perceived the smell of the burning food from the kitchen. He jumped off the chair. It was obviously too late to rescue his pot of rice. He had already made a very bad "burnt offering" of it. He switched off the stove, thanking God that the house was not set on fire. In his swift rescue effort, he struck the bottle of oil by the side of the stove. This resulted in multiple breakage and pandemonium in the kitchen. He hated himself for all these developments. He felt his life was upside down. The clean-up took almost an hour. He was more upset when he thought about his telephone conversations with Tracy on the probable reason why the Pastor needed to see them so urgently. He felt she was not very open and sounded a little secretive. His final assumption was that Tracy had decided to call it quits with him but wanted the Pastor to do the talking.

Some heat came upon him, and sweat gathered on his forehead. He was in this frenzy when the phone rang. He could not imagine who the caller was as the caller ID read, "blocked." He picked up the phone with mixed feelings and said: "Hello, God bless you!" Alas, it was an automated message trying to run a commercial. He was so angry that he banged the phone. Not quite thirty seconds, the phone rang again. He decided to ignore it and walked away to use the bathroom. He thought it was the commercial and if not "let the answering machine record the message," he decided. He was halfway through in the bathroom when he realized it was the voice of Tracy. He ran to the phone. She just hung up as he was about to pick the handset. The message was: "Bro Jimmy, it's been difficult to get through to you, please do not forget the appointment after the meeting tonight ... shalom." He checked on the caller ID; it was an unknown number. He guessed it was a public phone. He dialed the number; it rang endlessly until a passer-by picked it and said: "Hello, "this is a public phone."

Jimmy's baritone voice was not difficult for thy passer-by to identify. Incidentally, it was a brother from the church. "Is that Bro Jimmy?" "Yes, yes" he responded" Oh it's me Bro Ted," was the reply. Jimmy quickly said: "Is Sis Tracy around that place at all?" The reply was, "Yes, she just drove off. She only stopped by to make the call." In actual fact, she looked very worried. She said she forgot her cell phone at home, and that she was not able to get through to the person she stopped to call. She never said it was you."

The statement "she never said it was you" was like a gunshot. Jimmy felt dejected and rejected. He could not say any other word but "bye" to the man on the other end of the line. He paced around the house confused. He determined to get his mind together and ready for the worst.

The Wednesday service was very successful, though it went a little longer than the usual closing time. The Pastor quickly asked Jimmy and Tracy to meet with him in the office before any other person gained his attention. He told them he just must meet with them on the issue of their wedding date. The sigh from Jimmy was so loud that the Pastor had to question whether he was not expecting the discussion. His only response was, 'Thank God for Jesus." His countenance changed; he seemed to grow a little younger immediately. Certainly, his worries had made him look aged. The Pastor and Tracy focused their attention on him. He turned to see the face of Tracy. A face he had not been bold enough to look at with confidence before the casual but crucial statement of the Pastor. He could read love and approval expressed by Tracy. His worries were dispelled; he adjusted his seat as if to give the Pastor the approval to continue talking.

The wedding was fixed for the 30th of September. The Pastor suggested to the prospective couple to sort things out with their parents on all the necessary arrangements concerning the date and the traditional rites to be conducted. He then fixed three dates for monthly counseling sessions before the wedding day.

It was the practice of the A-Z Holiness Church to announce prospective weddings and names of the would-be couples at least two months before the wedding day. The Pastor promised to inform the church by the following Sunday. As promised the announcement of the wedding was made immediately after the worship service. The whole church went highly-strung. The noise was so much that the Pastor had to shout the congregation down to share the grace. The general statement:"...if anybody has a reason or rea- sons why these two should not be joined in holy matrimony, please make your objection known to the Pastor before the ...," was greeted with "No objection ..." It was very embarrassing for Jimmy but very gratifying for Tracy. It dawned on the two that they were now acknowledged as "couples without conjugal right." They were to put off the "old flames" if there be any.

CHAPTER TEN

THE OLD FLAMES

The announcement of the proposed wedding between Jimmy and Tracy was the talk of the town amongst the Christians both within and outside A-Z Holiness Church. Maurice was also surprised because he had for long doubted his perception, more so as he could hardly substantiate any good proof of a nuptial or spousal relationship between Jimmy and Tracy. He recalled how Tracy dismissed his perception with a wave of the hand. His heart was full of joy, and his soul justified that the Lord spoke to him about the relationship before its commencement. He determined to meet with Jimmy to ask some pertinent questions on how he came about his conviction to marry his "mother - in - the - 'Lord" (remember Maurice was one of Tracy's converts). A few days after the announcement of Jimmy's wedding date, it was obvious that his morale was boosted. The general opinion was that it was an achievement for him to marry the well-read and highly respected Sunday school superintendent. There were diverse opinions. To Maurice, it was a divine match and a unique relationship. He quickly made arrangements on how to have a dialogue with Bro Jimmy. Their meeting was very successful. To Maurice, it was very informative and educational. Jimmy was prepared to answer every one of his inquisitive questions. He had to explain what his prayer was while seeking the face of the Lord for a wife. He explained: "My principal prayer was that the Lord should give me a woman who will make me make heaven and will be good enough for my appreciation and admiration throughout life. It may interest you to know that I made mistakes initially, but the Lord rescued me in answer to my prayers." He had to narrate the story of how he rushed into a broken relationship with Jassy. With all modesty, he did not mention the name Jassy. The narrative really moved Maurice. With excitement, he questioned: "Sir, how did you become convinced that Sis. Tracy would be your God-given wife?"

He narrated his conviction and how the Pastor was involved. He looked into Maurice's eyes and said, "My beloved young man, do not base your conviction on sentiment and trivialities. You actually need to understand the depth and the meaning of the verse in the Bible: II Corinthians 4:18: "Since we consider and look not to the things that are seen but to the things that are unseen; for the things that are visible are temporal (brief and fleeting), but the things that are invisible are deathless and everlasting." Many men have fallen victim of external beauty, glamour, and superficiality. From what I have told you thus far you must have realized that I was not left out. It took time before I came to agree that "charm and grace are deceptive and beauty is vain [because it is not lasting], but a woman who reverently and worshipfully fears the Lord, she shall be praised" (Proverbs 31:30).

"When I came to understand this verse, I determined to focus more on godliness and contentment in my desire for a wife. It is my strong belief that Sis. Tracy is God's divine and perfect will for me in marriage."

Maurice paused and ruminated a while. He didn't know when he went into a soliloquy...   "Conviction, perfect will ... perfect will."

Jimmy cut in and said, "Yes! Perfect will. You need to realize the difference between a perfect will and permissive will."

"Please explain the difference," said Maurice.

"I am not going to take much of your time," declared Jimmy as he went on to explain: "Every will of God for man, perfect or permissive, will surely be challenged by the devil. Whenever a man is in the perfect will of God, there will always be enough grace to stand the challenges. The victory is always sure. There is no failure in the perfect will of God. This is what makes the difference."

"Could you please elucidate?" requested Maurice.

"You seem to have good listening ears with enough time and room to absorb facts," said Jimmy. They both laughed.

"You have spoken about your errors. That is why I want to know how to avoid such dangerous moments," asserted Maurice.

"It is good to have a teachable spirit. A teachable person will grow to become an asset while the gifted but not teachable may end up being deserted," said Jimmy.

"How then does one differentiate the perfect will from the permissive will especially at the inception or when decisions are to be made?" Maurice questioned.

In his reply, Jimmy said: "It takes a good knowledge of the word of God and a personal relationship with the Lord and the Holy Spirit to be able to discern the perfect will of God from his permissive will. Though they look alike when tested through the word of God and prayers the differences come clear. As long as man is yielded to the Spirit of God, he/she will be guided to be in the perfect will of God. Remember the statement of the Lord Jesus Christ, in John 16:13: "But when. He, the Spirit of Truth (the Truth-giving Spirit) comes; He will guide you into all the Truth (the whole, full Truth). For He will not speak His own message [on His own authority}; but He will tell whatever He hears [from the father; lie will give the message that has been given to Him}, and he will announce and declare to you the things that are to come [that will happen in the future]. "A permissive will is a will that satisfies the desires of man but falls short of God's expectation and desires for the individual. God does not wish evil for His children; neither does His perfect will. Jeremiah 29:11 states: "For I know the thoughts and the plans that I have for you, says the Lord, thoughts, and plans for welfare and peace and not for evil, to give you hope in your final outcome." You may need to read from the account of Balaam and Balak stated in Numbers chapters 22-25." Maurice reached for his Bible, but Jimmy reiterated that he should find a better time to study the account. He tried to summarize the passage, explaining the lust in the life of Balaam, the wicked resolution of Balak and God's deter-mination against Balaam. Stretching his right hand towards Maurice's shoulder as if to pull him a little closer, he said, "My beloved brother there is nothing as good as marrying God's divine will for one's life. It is better to remain single than to run into an irreversible marital relationship with a permissive or strange spouse. Let's read this verse of the Bible together."

He took his Bible, opened to Proverbs 25:24: "It is better to dwell in the corner of the housetop than to share a house with a disagreeing, quarrel some, and scolding woman." Let's see a more explanatory verse on the same issue." He opened to Proverbs 21:9 and read, running his index finger through the lines to call for better attention, "It is better to dwell in a corner of the housetop [on the flat oriental roof, exposed to all kinds of weather than in a house shared with a nagging, quarrel some, and fault scolding woman." "In my own under-standing, this verse of the scripture implies that it is better to face the challenges of being single than to live with a spouse who is not God's perfect will."

Maurice took a deep breath. He looked at Jimmy's face and Said: "Sir, you have turned my life around. Please don't hesitate henceforth to treat me as your son in the Lord." He humorously added: "Especially now that you are taking my mother-in-Christ to the altar" They both laughed. After a short prayer, they parted. It was one of Maurice's best tutorials ever. As he was about leaving, he turned to Jimmy and asked whether he knew Associate Pastor (Dr.) Dickson. 'Very well," said Jimmy. "He is back in town," Maurice asserted. He was in our office a few weeks ago. I am surprised he has not come to fellowship with us in the church. It will be nice meeting him again. He was very helpful when we first met. I guess Sis. Tracy must have met with him," Jimmy responded. "Sure" exclaimed Maurice. Jimmy gave him a handshake. They parted.

The news of Tracy and Jimmy's proposed wedding was not well-received by Dickson. His lustful thought towards Tracy still gripped his mind. His visit to Tracy's office was to ignite the smothering "old flame." He narrated to her the plight of his final clinical housemanship which was unsuccessful. His presentation was a call for sympathy with a flavor of passion. His insinuations were obvious as his lust was conspicuous in his facial expression. Tracy got the message but chose to taunt him, probably to convict him of sin. She offered him a list of the prospective wedding gifts and said: "I guess you are here to pick one of the most expensive gifts on the list." They both smiled. His response was a little weird as he said, "The best gift I have for you is my body, spirit, and soul to offer any service required," trying to make his insinuation sound spiritual but ambiguous. Tracy understood his statement as a demand for an immoral relationship. Her heart bled as she recalled their immoral discussions especially her tele-fornication which a few months back almost destroyed her spiritual life. It was difficult for her to be assertive in her understanding of Dickson's intention. She knew that any entertainment of his intention would put her into a difficult situation. She decided to sound a little offensive. She said: "I guess you may need to give more attention to overcoming your academic and spiritual failures than us this time around." The statement really offended Dickson. He felt he was called a failure. He realized that the gap expected between him and Tracy had been grossly eroded. He knew he had lost his dignity and respect. However, it was difficult for him to charge Tracy for any insult; rather he gave an enigmatic smile as he said:

"I am down, but not out, I will surely overcome my failures in life."

He was really shocked from his head to his toes. His legs almost wobbled as he left Tracy's office. In actual fact, he was not offered a cup of tea this time around. The departure was very unceremonial; no mention was made about any further meeting. Tracy was very modest as she saw him off to his car. She sounded a little sarcastic as she said: "30th of September is the day. I hope you meet Bro. Jimmy before then. Have a safe journey home."

She returned into her office with a sense of guilt of being probably rude and disrespectful. As she sat in her seat, she was comforted by the Holy Spirit. She heard a voice in her spirit that said, "I bailed you out." She felt well pleased. It was a nice way to say NO.

Associate Pastor Dickson returned home dejected but unrepentant his conscience had been seared with a hot iron. He was marked out for destruction by the devil. He must have forgotten how he offended the devil in those good old early days of his life in Christ. He forgot that the devil neither forgives nor forgets. He had lost the prompting by the Holy Spirit. He did not remember the statement of the Lord Jesus in John 14:30: "I will not talk with you much more, for the prince (evil genius, ruler) of the world is coming. And he has no claim on Me [He has nothing in common with Me; there is nothing in Me that belongs to him, and he has no power over Me]." He was prompted to call on an old acquaintance he met at the church where he now fellowshipped. His telephone discussion was perfectly fueled by the devil. It was very animating and slightly romantic. They both agreed to have further discussions after the next meeting in the church.

Debby had tested HIV positive after she was raped at a "sleepover party." The experience was irreversible. The traumatic experience got her more committed to the cause of Christ especially as she was very conscious of the fact that her days on earth may not be for too long. She was actively involved in many activities in the church and was all out to please the Lord. Her composure portrayed her as a very gentle and easy- going lady. Her plight had submerged her pride. Her "humiliation" was generally taken for humility. She had no other burning desire than to make heaven at the end of her "un-timely death."

After the church service, Dickson engaged Debby in a very intimate discussion. His inordinate and lustful interest was obvious but cleverly presented for his personal safety and the protection of his image and integrity as an ordained minister of the gospel. However, his insinuations were clearly understood by Debby. She was taken aback by the idea. Her reasons were based on her resolution about heaven, and the integrity and respect she had for Pastor Dickson. She declined his offer of dinner for the evening. Dickson questioned her reasons, but she chose to remain determined. The meeting ended without a word of prayer except for this note from Dickson "God is a God of mercy". Though the phrase did not have any direct bearing in line with the discussion it was Satan-inspired to lure Debby into sin. Debby was very troubled by the meaning of the phrase: "God is a God of mercy." She was fighting its implication as impressed in her mind when the devil twisted I John I: 8-9 in attempt to indict her. The text reads: "If we say we have no sin [refusing to admit that we are sinners], we delude and lead ourselves astray, and the Truth [which the Gospel presents] is not in us (does not dwell in our hearts]. If we [freely] admit that we have sinned and confess our sins, He is faithful and just [true to His own nature and promises] and will forgive our sins [dismiss our lawlessness] and [continuously] cleanse us from all unrighteousness [everything not in conformity to His will in purpose, thought, and action]" She admitted that she could not claim to be without sin.

The devil then questioned her on what gave her the impression that she would not be forgiven if she fell into any sin, especially if she confessed it to the Lord. She remembered some of the statements made by Dickson during their private discussion. She could not get over this particular one which he claimed to have heard in a movie: "If you take a prospective picture which may not be desirable, refuse to develop the film." She knew what Dickson was putting across. Though she ignored it then, now it had become the devil's springboard. In her thoughts she was cautioned by the Holy Spirit to realize that technology has advanced beyond the idea of not developing a film, the cameras are now digital. All images are registered without the use of film. She interpreted the influx as a caution that sins cannot be hidden; they are automatically registered in the presence of the Lord. She remembered the Bible passage that reads: "And not a creature exists that is concealed from His sight, but all things are opened and exposed, naked and defenseless to the eye of Him with whom we have to do." She pitied Dickson for his ignorance of her. Dickson was asking for both physical and probably eternal death. She decided not to consent, but her passion overrode reason. The devil built on her lustful passion especially as she was disappointed by Associate Pastor Dickson. She was given the impression that immorality may not necessarily be absurd among the so-called men and women of God.

The battle was raging in her mind. The devil reminded her that "God is a God of mercy". Suddenly she remembered that the Bible says in Hebrew 10:23: "So let us seize and hold fast and retain without wavering the hope we cherish and confess and our acknowledgement of it, for He who promised is reliable (sure) and faithful to His word; 26-27 For if we go on deliberately and willingly sinning after once acquiring the knowledge of the Truth, there is no longer any sacrifice left to atone for [our] sins (no further offering to which to look forward. [There is nothing left for us then] but a kind of awful and fearful prospect and expectation of divine judgment and the fury of burning wrath and indignation which will consume those who put themselves in opposition [to God]. She remembered one of the Sunday-school memory verses: "For It is impossible (to restore and bring again to repentance) those who have been once for all enlightened, who have consciously tasted the heavenly gift and have become sharers of the Holy Spirit, and have felt how good the Word of God is and the mighty powers of the age and world to come. If they then deviate from the faith and turn away from their allegiance - [it is impossible] to bring them back to repentance for (because, while as long as) they nail upon the cross the Son of God afresh holding [Him] up to contempt and shame and public disgrace. Heb. 6: 4 "She determined not to consent to Dickson's insinuations, but she did not remember to pray that the Holy Spirit should help her determination. She was very confident in herself. She forgot Zechariah 4:6: "Saying not by might, nor by power, but by My Spirit of Whom the oil is a symbol, says the Lord of hosts."

Debby had had at least a week of battle on the seed planted in her mind by the devil through Pastor Dickson. Her lack of prayers was her greatest weakness. She was about preparing to leave for church when the phone rang. It was Dickson. The conversation was brief and casual. He offered to give her a ride as he was not too far from her. To Debby, it was a good privilege. She believed it would save her time and money which she would have spent on public transport. A few minutes later, the doorbell rang. Alas, it was Dickson. He came in with some bags of shopping. Debby intercepted him with the question: "Sir, what are all these?" The answer was "All for you including me." To Debby, the phrase "including me" sounded very ambiguous. Could it mean: "The items are for both of us" or "all for you, and my very self for you as well?" Subsequent discussions proved it all. Debby was "swept off her feet." It was all over. After the die was cast, Debby felt very sad but was comforted by Dickson. With tears rolling down her cheeks she asked: "Are we still going to church ... how we shall face the Lord?" With little or no remorse for his preposterous act, he replied: "... but neither of us is the preacher for tonight." This reply was a deadly blow on Debby. She burst into tears. She felt she had fallen into the hands of a "real devil." She could not believe that the associate pastor could be that insensitive to the Holy Spirit. She was very repentant. She advised Dickson to leave her house. She sent him packing with this note: "I pray I am able to forgive myself after this sinful act and unfaithfulness. I may have to confess this to the Pastor. My other prayer is that this act is not "fruitful," I mean that I do not become pregnant..." After a very deep sigh, she said "I hope you are free of "me.""

Dickson did not clearly understand the last phrase. He, however, pleaded that the secret is concealed between them both. The matter eventually got to the Pastor and some brethren. Debby did not become pregnant; however, the HIV was already passed on to Dickson. His ministerial image was severely damaged; the fact of the case became the talk of the town. His Pastor had to compare notes with Pastor King. He was viewed as a devil by most of the brethren. He could not concentrate on his studies. He became depressed and looked undernourished. He got completely shattered when his blood test proved HIV positive.

His state of depression deteriorated into demonic oppression. It was the beginning of the end for him.

The news of Dickson's scandal really disturbed Tracy. She could not get over the still small voice of the Holy Spirit: "I bailed you out." She was so troubled that she felt the only way to have her peace was to share her "close shave" with someone. She decided to share it with her fiancés Jimmy. They both pitied Associate Pastor Dickson. Several questions ran through their minds which included: 'When did he actually fall? How did he fall? For how long had he fallen? Did he seek any help by confessing his lustful imaginations? How many sisters has he defiled? Will God for-give him? Will he forgive himself? Will the brethren still accept him?" Thinking of all these questions..., they both went on their knees to intercede for him. It was their belief that the Lord would forgive him. Their worry was that the brethren might not easily forgive or forget his act. He had to live with the scar. The Bible says "But whoever commits adultery with a woman lacks heart and understanding [moral principle and prudence]; he who does it is destroying his own life. Wounds and disgrace will he get, and his reproach will not be wiped away," Proverbs 6:32-33.

Tracy was of the opinion that they should find time to visit Associate Pastor Dickson to express their concern for him at such a crucial and critical moment. The obvious fact was that he had become an odium and a religious repugnance to believers and unbelievers alike. Jimmy with some expression of grief on his face turned to Tracy and said, "Some months ago, who could have thought that people will die tum away from Associate Pastor Dickson. He was always there for everybody. Today he is wounded, down and deserted. This is what scares me about our brethren. Now, everybody talks about his obnoxious acts, forgetting all those good qualities from which we have all benefited." With a deep sigh and eyes laden with tears Tracy said, "Ours is the only army where the wounded are shot dead ... could it be that our brethren go too far on II Timothy 3:5: " For [although] they hold a form of piety [true religion], they deny and reject and are strangers to the power of it [their conduct belies the genuineness of their profession]. Avoid [all] such people [turn away from them]. "With her left thumb she gleaned the tears that blurred her vision as she retorted, "..it could not be the fulfillment of Ezekiel 18:23-24: "Have I any pleasure in the death of the wicked? Says the Lord and not rather that he should turn from his evil way and return [to his God] and live? But if the righteous man turns away from his righteousness and commits iniquity and does according to all the abominations that the wicked man does, shall he live? None of his righteous deeds which he has done shall be remembered. In his trespass that he has trespassed and in his sin that he has sinned, in them shall he die. "Jimmy cut in to say: "My dear sister, I think our best bet is to make sure we keep our stand in the Lord and be faithful to the end. Remember what Apostle Paul said in 1 Corinthians 10:12: "Therefore let anyone who thinks he stands [who feels sure that he has a steadfast mind and is standing firm], take heed lest he falls [into sin]." Taking a very deep breath, Tracy said: "May -God- help- us."

Jimmy was very sorrowful when he remembered the appeal of his pastor in one of his sermons: "Therefore, my dear ones, as you have always obeyed [my suggestions], so now, not only [with the enthusiasm you would show] in my presence but much more because I am absent, work out (cultivate, carry out to the goals, and fully complete) your own salvation with reverence and awe and trembling (self-distrust, with serious caution, tenderness of conscience, watchfulness against temptation, timidly shrinking from whatever might offend God and discredit the name of Christ." Philippians 2: 12. Deep in the heart of Tracy was her sense of guilt. In her imagination she thought could it be that she was responsible for the predicaments of Dickson or could it be that he had been promiscuous before meeting with her. She pleaded for forgiveness of sin. Her guilt was evident on her face. Jimmy beholding her gloomy face questioned: do you have any special reason why you are extremely devastated by the plight of

Associate pastor Dickson?" "Not really I was just meditating about the Bible passage; I Peter 5:8 which reads: "Be well balanced (temperate, sober of mind), be vigilant and cautious at all times; for that enemy of yours, the devil, roams around like a lion roaring (in fierce hunger), seeking someone to seize upon and devour." Regrettably, she added," I have always thought that Associate Pastor Dickson was a very sound and established Christian" Though they thought it necessary to visit Dickson, they did not feel competent enough to counsel a Pastor. It was however agreed that their visit would be a proof of love and acceptance. They also agreed to encourage Pastor King to accept his former associate at a time as this. At least the Bible says "Iron sharpens iron so a man sharp-ens the countenance of his friend," "said Tracy. "Are they friends?" Jimmy asked. "I should think so, maybe Pastor needs our counsel," 'Tracy concluded

They both nodded in agreement, but could not understand how to go about the counseling.

CHAPTER ELEVEN

PREMARITAL COUNSELING

Day One

As the wedding date drew near, it became very mandatory for Pastor King to create time out of his hectic schedule to meet with Jimmy and Tracy. He could have delegated this responsibility to any other minister in the church, but because of the level of ministerial involvement of the prospective couple themselves, he had to take it up personally. The first meeting was very brief but loaded. The session was opened with a short prayer after which the Pastor said:

"I am quite aware that you have had some heated arguments on issues where your opinions were at variance, however, may I advise you to realize that you have some more weeks to disagree. You had better disagree now in order to agree than to agree to disagree. As at now, you may choose to pray unilaterally without any hindrance. Very soon you may need more of corporate prayers and agreement to make things happen. Note what the Bible says in

Matthew 18:19: " Again I tell you, if two of you on earth agree [harmonize together, make a symphony together] about whatever [anything and everything] they may ask, it will come to pass and be done for them by My father in heaven.

"Please realize the importance of your agreement. Amos 3:3 reads: "Do two walk together except they make an appointment and have agreed?"

Jimmy raised up his right hand as if to object to the Scripture the Pastor had just quoted. The look on Tracy's face was a counter-reaction. The Pastor asked: "Sir what do you have to say?" "It's on this issue of disagreement," replied Jimmy. "What about?" The Pastor questioned. Jimmy looked at the face of Tracy as if to receive an approval to speak.

"I mean disagreement," he reiterated. Staring at him, 'Tracy said:

"Is it a new word?" They all laughed. Jimmy felt he was edged in by Tracy.

"But you know our disagreement," he calmly charged.

With a smile, Tracy replied, "Not just one." Jimmy was taken aback.

With his eyes wide-open as if to desire a more (clearer) vision, he asked,

"How many?"

"A catalog," replied Tracy. "Pastor I need rescue," Jimmy pleaded. They all laughed. The Pastor turning to Jimmy said. "I can guess that you have a particular issue on which you very strongly disagree with Sis Tracy, could you please just mention it to save time?" "So that I can also bring in my own points of disagreements," stressed Tracy. "I hope today is not the judgment day," responded Jimmy. "Not at all," said the Pastor. "It is my safe place to talk," asserted Tracy. They all laughed again. Jimmy, turning to the Pastor said: "It is on this issue of female circumcision. "Tracy was surprised but not disappointed that Jimmy brought the issue up again. Her surprise was clearly expressed with her mouth agape. The Pastor was startled, and his mind disconcerted because he had never handled the matter of female circumcision as a point of conflict between prospective couples. He was however mature enough to conceal his discomfiture.

"I must commend the sincerity of you both. I have enjoyed your styles of expression of your minds and the differences in your opinions. It is my belief that you will make a perfect couple in the near future ..." the Pastor expressed.

This opinion of the Pastor gave Jimmy a little more sense of security. It allayed the fear that was building up in his mind. The Pastor went on: "I do not intend to discuss any cultural practice on this issue but only the Biblical principles as commanded by God. In my limited knowledge of the Scripture, God did not command the circumcision of female but male children born unto Abraham and his household to which we Christians belong, Genesis 17:9-14. May I advise that you should not allow any unscriptural practice or culture to create any problem in your relationship? It should be realized that female circumcision is a primitive and cruel act. It is nothing but genital mutilation designed to rob the female sex of the fullness of their sexuality. This is one of the factors that lead to frigidity (female lack of responsiveness or interest in the act of sex); it has destroyed many marriages and caused divorce in some cases (with its attendant problems on the children and the society as a whole)."

Jimmy, trying to justify female circumcision said, "If a young lady is less sexually sensitive, she will be able to keep her virginity." His argument was beaten hands down by Tracy who un-equivocally said: "I disagree. Virginity, fidelity, piety cannot be destroyed by sexual sensitivity but infatuation and fantasy. It is the knowledge of the word of God and personal discipline that can keep any- body pure and holy." With her right hand on her chest as if she were to read a pledge or take an oath she said, "To the glory of God, I am thirty-two years plus and I am still a virgin."

The Pastor trying to instill some order having sensed a little tension in the voice and expression of Tracy said: "Please let us learn discipline by talking only at my order." Tracy immediately tendered an apology.

The Pastor said: "I thank God for the lives of the two of you, for your sincerity, purity, and holiness. You have the question and the answer with you. On this issue of our discussion, legalism is not the solution but the yield of the individual to the Holy Spirit. Please be wise enough to keep the counsel of the Lord. May I advise that you should not consent to female circumcision if you do not intend to add more to the ever-increasing family problems and divorce. The frigidity of some women in marriage has compelled some men to fall into the temptation of the devil to try sex with other women whom he knew were not circumcised. Some of them had better response or experience and thereby refused to return to their legitimate wives." Tracy cogitated and confidently stared at Jimmy. The Pastor quickly cautioned: 'There is no victor or vanquished, this is the key to resolving disagreements and conflicts." Tracy turned, trying to cuddle Jimmy to accept the "verdict." She smiled as she said, "when you are 'certified' you will have the unadulterated, unmutilated bride." The Pastor raised his hand in objection and humorously said, "A few weeks too early." They all laughed.

"I guess we have to defer further discussions till when next we meet," the Pastor suggested.

The meeting was rounded off with a short prayer. The next session was fixed for the morning of the following Saturday.

Day Two

Tracy was not delighted with a Saturday morning appointment, but she had no choice especially as the wedding day was fast approaching. She desired that the meeting should not belong. She arrived on time at the office, but Jimmy was nowhere to be found. The Pastor decided to honor an unscheduled appointment before the arrival of Jimmy who came almost an hour late. Tracy was really cross. She blushed. Her displeasure was evident in her countenance. She chose not to look at the direction of Jimmy as he rushed into the office trying to avoid a drench in the rain, which started about fifteen minutes before his arrival. In his rush, he slipped and fell. It was his crash that caused Tracy to turn around. She was shocked to see the "six-footer" flat on the floor. It was not a laughing matter because of a fairly deep cut sustained as a result of hitting the side of his head on an unrounded edge of one of the office furniture. Her anger was dispelled when she saw the outflow of blood from Jimmy's head. Jimmy was actually in pain, he had a twisted and sprained ankle. He tried to play brave, but his agony was evident on his face. He was given first aid treatment by the office staff.

Everybody around was very sympathetic, Tracy was empathetic. She was almost crying her eyes out as she held Jimmy's head, asking: "I hope you are alright ... are you okay Bro Jimmy?" His silence was of great concern. She got him to sit on a seat at the extreme end of the office. It was difficult' to agree that Tracy was not confused about how to handle the situation. She pulled Jimmy to herself with his head across her breasts as if he were a dying baby. Waiting for the arrival of the ambulance was more scary and traumatic. The arrival of the ambulance was a little hindered by the traffic as a result of the heavy downpour. At the sound of the ambulance's siren, the Pastor came out of his office. He was shocked by the sight, disappointed that the secretary did not inform him about the development (accident) of that magnitude. The secretary tendered an apology. Though the Pastor was disturbed by the posture of Jimmy and Tracy, he was however overwhelmed and traumatized by the sight of blood. He stylishly went to lift Jimmy' off Tracy. It was timely; the ambulance had arrived. Though some of the brethren had prayed, the Pastor also offered a prayer before the ambulance whisked Jimmy away. Tracy's offer to go with him in the ambulance was turned down by paramedical staff. They felt her tears were of no help and may have a more psychological effect on Jimmy. In her determination, she drove her car, accompanied by two brethren. The raced behind the fast-moving ambulance as it blared its siren.

Jimmy was given immediate attention. Every necessary medical test was conducted. He was stable, but the doctor decided he should be admitted for observation, especially for the impact of the head injury. The doctor's decision did not go well with either Tracy or Jimmy. They, however, agreed not to decide against medical advice. Tracy was sitting by Jimmy's bedside when the Pastor came in. The smile on her face was very encouraging to the Pastor who was quite agitated by the development. He sat at the foot of the bed as he humorously said: "This is not where we agreed to meet." They all laughed, he turned to Jimmy and asked, 'Bro Jimmy, what actually happened?" He narrated the story of how he tried to avoid the rain and slipped. The Pastor paused for a while and said: "If you had come at the appropriate time of our appointment you would have beaten the rain. Anyway, that was not to make you feel guilty."

"What actually caused your delay?" questioned Tracy. Jimmy was reluctant to say he went to visit somebody through whom he was to send some items to his mother back in his home- country. He was quite aware that his exceptional love and con-cern for his mother had in the past threatened their courtship. The mere mention of it seemed to change Tracy's mood. The Pastor by experience was able to understand what was going on. With a good sense of humor he said: "Now that you are going to get married, (looking into Jimmy's eyes), you will have someone to take better care of your mother." With an enigmatic smile, Tracy said: "I guess she will be our first baby."

The Pastor with a warm smile asserted: "Your 'second mother', and you will take good care of her!" "If he allows me," responded Tracy.

While the other two brethren were away on an errand, the Pastor engaged the would-be couple on the subject of sharing and caring. His first statement generated little or no smile. There was tension in the air. Tracy was distraught. She attributed Jimmy's accident to his priority for his mother at the expense of their appointment with the Pastor. The Pastor in his attempt to make room for a mood swing said: "I was going to share with you on sharing and caring, I expected you to have the theory class before the practical. Based on the mood I met the two of you when I came out of my office, it was obvious that part of the practical had preceded the theory. I guess it was an opportunity for undue closeness."

"Not really," replied Jimmy.

"I can understand," responded the Pastor. They all laughed. Turning to Tracy, the Pastor said: "I must commend your bravery and care for Bro Jimmy. I watched your speed after the ambulance; it gave me the impression that you must be an experienced cab driver."

The statement actually dispelled Tracy's moody expression as she responded with a burst of fairly wide laughter which must have disturbed some other patients. The Pastor signaled to caution that they were in a hospital. Jimmy turned to the Pastor, mused a little and said: "I am very confident of the fact that she loves me."

"I wish you love me as much in return," responded Tracy. The Pastor cut in to add, teasing Tracy, "Probably a little more than his mum!" "Exactly," she replied. They all laughed. Jimmy interrupted the laughter with the statement: "Well, you are already working for it..." "By putting your head on her chest," the Pastor interjected. "Oh no!" said Jimmy. "I do understand," replied the Pastor. They all laughed.

By now the ground was well-prepared for some in-depth factual discussions. The Pastor said: "Let me teach you a secret of matrimonial bliss. It is called: "PARENTAL EXCHANGE." I am very much aware of the fact that you both love your parents very seriously. Your best bet for a happy marital relationship will be to exchange them. It simply implies that you," focusing his gaze on Jimmy, "will put the interest and well-being of your parents at the mercies of your darling, Tracy." "I hope he trusts me that much ..." Tracy sarcastically interrupted. "When I was very young I was taught not to interrupt the elders when they talk." She got the message and immediately tendered an apology. She, however, took it as a more serious, charge against her parents, ethics and her personal demeanor. To Tracy, the statement was very indicting and insinuated her lack of some basic home training. Her inner thought was evident in her countenance. She became very petulant and crabby.

The Pastor immediately realized the reversion in the climate of the room. There was no doubt Tracy was very sensitive especially to comments that touched on her parents. To make for his unintended assault on Tracy's good mood, the Pastor turned to her with a glow in his eyes as if to charge or inspire the dying radiance on her face with the overflow of his humorous countenance. For the very first time ever he cuddled Tracy. This expression was overwhelming; she burst into tears. She mumbled as she sobbed," Sir, I never meant to be rude to you, neither did I least imagine any undue familiarity or take you for granted. I guess you did not mean to insult my parents or charge them for not giving me proper up-b-bringing as it were." She hooted. It was a very emotional moment; the Pastor had his hands full.

The Pastor, with a tone that almost suggested hopelessness pulled Tracy to his side and said: "Sis Tracy, far be it that I should charge you or your parents for lack of ethics. That would not have implied the failure of your biological parents but for me as your spiritual father. You have been a model and modest lady in the church; I never meant to hurt you." Turning to Jimmy whom he was trying to impress, he realized he was more depressed and deflated than a punctured balloon. With a passionate composure and forced a smile the Pastor said to Jimmy,

"The scenario of this day has proved to be more practical than theoretical. By now you should be able to appreciate how damaging a derogatory comment can be to your "darling- heart."

"You are both blessed," asserted the Pastor. "I guess you both have realized how painful and damaging it could be when you take very personal issues that relate to your parents in your marital relationship. If you both agree to cater to each other's concerns and interest in your parents, your home will experience such peace that you can never imagine."

Just as a kindergarten pupil would have done, Jimmy put up his right hand to gain the 'Pastor's approval of his intended interruption. The Pastor laughed as Tracy humorously said: "Good boy in a cortina pair of shoe," which simply implies "BACK TO SCHOOL." (Cortina-shoes were then popularly advertised for pupils returning to school). The Pastor commented, "Well...I have always been a 'teacher, thank you for reminding me of my root." They all laughed.

The Pastor signaled to Jimmy to make his comment or ask his question.

"Does "Parental Exchange" mean I no longer have free access to my parents when we get married?" This question did not win the admiration of Tracy who had always seen Jimmy as "a boy in an adult frame." She had in the past teased Jimmy to travel back home for a suck. The Pastor realized the sensitivity of the question and how much wisdom was required in giving an answer. His reply was: "You do not lose your parents but rather gain two more and in addition one regent of them all, your lovable beauty queen."

He gestured towards Tracy who responded with a broad smile.

"That is me, "Tracy asserted. It was all smiles.

Facing Tracy, the Pastor charged: "Now that you know that Mummy is "Jimmy's treasured possession's it will behoove you to take good care of her. "In my own interest and peace," Tracy consented. Laying her hands on Jimmy's wounded head, and smiling, she said: "I promise to care for mummy than you could ever have done. I will love her almost as I love you." Tracy's statement generated a lot of warmth in Jimmy's heart. His face brightened with a glow of fulfillment in his eyes. The Pastor surreptitiously added, "Dr. Tracy will definitely treat Bro Jimmy better. No doubt, he would have recovered better in her "clinic." I guess Bro Jimmy was brought here in error."

The Pastor, as usual, encouraged the would-be married couple to base everything in their relationship on the word of God. He cautioned them on the power of the spoken word by reading from his Bible, Ephesians 4:29-32: "Let no foul or polluting language nor evil word nor unwholesome or worth- less-talk [ever] come out of your mouth, but only such speech as is good, and beneficial to the spiritual progress of others, as is fitting to the need and the occasion that it may be a blessing and give grace [God's favor] to those who hear it, and do not grieve the Holy Spirit of God [do not offend or vex or sadden him] by whom you are saved [marked, branded as God's own, secured] for the day of redemption [of final deliverance through Christ from evil and consequences of sin]. Let all bitterness and indignation and wrath (passion, rage, bad temper] and resentment [anger, animosity and quarreling [brawling, clamor, contention] and slander [evil speaking, abusive or blasphemous language] be banished from you with all malice [spite, ill will or baseness of any kind]. And become useful and helpful and kind to one another, tenderhearted (compassionate, understanding, loving hearted], forgiving one another [readily and freely], as God in Christ forgave you.";

Romans 12:9-10: Let your love be sincere [a real thing]; hate what is evil [loathe all ungodliness, turn in horror from wickedness], but hold fast to that which is good. Love one another with brotherly affection [as members of one family}, giving precedence and showing honor to one another." After a short prayer, the Pastor took his leave. In his parting statement, he said: "Bro Jimmy, please realize that diverse spirits operate in a hospital environment. Be strong and of good courage. Take charge till You are discharged."

Day Three

The Pastor had been very busy. He could do nothing than to fix the third and final counseling session in his own home. To Jimmy, it was a great honor. He also felt it would be a wonderful time, trusting that the Pastor's wife would prepare a good dish to break his monotony of "bachelors' companions" (snacks and bread). He chose to arrive early for the appointment. He was very disappointed when he drove past the Pastor's wife at the entrance of the street. His first thought was:

"No show it's going to be another soda (soft drink and snacks) meeting." On his arrival at the Pastor's living-room, his nostrils were greeted with the tantalizing sweet aroma from the kitchen. He salivated but could not make a demand to satisfy his taste-bud or exercise his jaws. He felt disappointed as he gulped down a chunk of accumulated enzymes. He determined to play on Tracy's intelligence to put his desire across. His Continual wait for Tracy's arrival was a taunt on his hunger to satisfy his appetite.

Tracy had a little delay but still managed to arrive on time, at 6.30 pm. as requested by the Pastor. 'Tracy's arriving just on time gave no room for-Jimmy to play on her intelligence at all. The Pastor came out of his study just as Tracy walked in. His comment was a big relief for Jimmy. "Mummy was aware of your coming; she has made adequate provision for your dinner. I guess you will leave here in ".full tank."" Jimmy trying to suggest his state of hunger, humorously raised up his right hand while he put the left on his belly, singing the song; 'Fill my cup Lord, I lift it up Lord, come and quench this thirsting of my soul, bread of heaven, fill me till I want no more, fill my cup, fill it Lord, and make me whole". The Pastor joined him religiously not getting the message. Though Tracy got the message, she couldn't educate the Pastor on Jimmy's predicament and desire. They sang the song about six times. Jimmy did a good singing with his baritone voice but could not understand the "insensitivity" of the Pastor to his starving appetite. The Pastor rounded off the singing session with a word of prayer.

The discussion commenced, the Pastor realized that Jimmy was not looking very radiant. He jokingly said: "I hope you are not feeling disturbed by the inquisitive cry (who-who -who) of the owl in the woods be- hind the house?" Tracy who had been a little agitated by the cry of the owl questioned the Pastor if the superstition attached to the cry of an owl is of any relevance to a Christian. The Pastor responded by saying: "The owl is traditionally believed to be an evil or mystic bird that cries "who-who-who is next to die." However, its cry is irrelevant to a child of God." He quoted Colossians 3:3: "For [as far as this world is concerned] you have died, and your [new real life is hidden with Christ in God.";

John 10:27-30: "The sheep that are My own hear and are listening to My voice, and I know them) and they follow Me. And! Give them eternal life, and they shall never lose it or perish throughout the ages. (To all eternity they shall never by any means be destroyed.) And no one is able to snatch them out of My hand. My Father, Who has given them to Me, is greater and mightier than all (else);

and no one is able to snatch [them] out of the Father's hand 1, and the Father are One.";

Psalm 18:17: "He delivered me from my strong enemy and from those who hated and abhorred me, for they were too strong for me." To back his assertion.

The Pastor's reassurance and Bible references actually put confidence into 'Tracy's spirit and allayed the trepidation that was already pervading her soul over the ill health of her father. Jimmy's reaction to the Pastor's statement was quite different. He said:

"I guess I never heard the inquisitive cry of the owl, probably because of the hole or hollow and emptiness of my stomach." At this juncture, the Pastor realized that the expression of perturbation and turbulence on the face of Jimmy was not of a spiritual attack but the result of hunger.

There was no doubt the three of them were operating at different frequencies and probably not in the same "realm." The Pastor requested Tracy to enter the kitchen and serve the table before they actually got into the business of the day. He humorously said: 'let's fulfill the scripture, James 2:15-18: "If a brother or sister is poorly clad and lacks food for each day, and one of you says to him, good-bye! Keep [yourself] warm and well fed, without giving him the necessities for the body, what good does that do? So always faith, if it does not have works [deeds and actions of obedience to back it up}, by itself is destitute of power [non-operative, dead]. But someone will say [to you then}, you [say you] have faith, and 1 has [good} works.

Now you show me your [alleged} faith apart from any [good] works [if you can} and I by [good] works [of obedience} will show you my faith."
Jimmy with every air of relief and liberty said: "God bless you, Sir, I came straight from work. That was why I raised the song; "fill my cup, Lord.""
"Oh no!" the Pastor exclaimed. 'I thought you were being very spiritual under divine inspiration. I am very sorry I did not get your message in song."
They all laughed.

Tracy did good work at serving the table. It was a charming dinner. The Pastor later affirmed, "I am very sure that Bro Jimmy can hear the whisper of the sparrow, though a few minutes ago he could not hear the hooting of the owl.
Sis Tracy, please take note." Laughter. Tracy, teasing Jimmy, chipped in:

"I never realized that hunger could make a man deaf." "This is why you cannot afford to fail in your domestic chemistry in the kitchen," retorted the Pastor. "Exactly," affirmed Jimmy. They all laughed.

It was time actually to start the discussion of the day. "Let me, first of all, congratulate you on the success of the traditional rites and final agreement of your parents on your proposed wedding. The short notes and pictures were delivered by my secretary." Tracy expressed surprise because she was not aware that Jimmy would be eager to send the pictures to the Pastor. She had felt terrible about some of the expressions on the faces of Jimmy's parents as caught by the camera. They showed little or no excitement, their expressions were expressive of their opinion that Tracy had successfully turned the mind of their son against the Islamic religion. She felt very insecure having them as in-laws. She had earlier called the attention of Jimmy to the fact that his parents did not accept her as their would-be daughter-in-law. She had been reassured by Jimmy that her gift to his mother had really won her over. Jimmy's reassurance had an impact because his mother had always sounded very friendly over the phone. It was his father that never had on any occasion tried to engage Tracy in a dialogue. The conversion of Jimmy into Christianity was one of the most significant blows of his life as he was top notch in the Islamic circle.

Tracy turned to the Pastor and said: "Sir, I guess the copies of the picture sent to you are not as scary as the one I have seen." The Pastor smiled as he responded: "Parental Exchange." "Yes, that is what makes it scarier," asserted Tracy. There was no doubt that the pictures really betrayed Jimmy. He would have had excuses or other suspicions if they had not been sent by his younger sister. This betrayal made him determined to love his wife and stick to her come what may. He felt the vindictive and unforgiving spirit which he sensed in his parents since he gave his life to Jesus was being vented and directed at Tracy. It was a feeling he could not express. He was becoming very emotional when he turned to the Pastor and said: "Sir, trust me, I will forever love my wife. These pictures have done her the best good ever. She would ever live to thank God for these pictures." His statement was very inspiring; it ignited radiance in the atmosphere. The Pastor was very impressed. Tracy emotionally responded: "Bro Jimmy, I promise to lavish my love on your parents because of you. As long as I have your love, they will forever know and enjoy our love. I believe our love will win them for Christ." "AMEN," Jimmy shouted.

The Pastor quickly zeroed in on the spiritual climate to register the love pledges in the realm of the spirit. He held their hands and prayed: "Father let these statements of your children become an everlasting covenant in Jesus' name." They both said a heartfelt "Amen."

After the prayer, the Pastor went on: "I quite appreciate the blessing of the Lord in your lives. I know you can afford to bear the cost of your wedding without any financial support from your parents or brethren. I still need to advise you to be very careful about how much dependent you may be when it comes to planning your wedding. Experience shows that most of those who give heavy financial support or play very influential roles in the whole issue tend to become very imperialistic at the end of the day. They may attempt to dictate what you should do in your new home. May I appeal that you do not bite off more than you can chew." He paused for a while, there was silence. They both looked at each other's face as if to ask what next? The Pastor went on: "All things being equal, by now every necessary arrangement must have been made about your reception ... Here is good news:"The Bishop, Pastor Amos has agreed to take the sermon at your wedding." It was very incredible news. Jimmy and Tracy sank into their chairs with their hands on their chins. Jimmy invariably raised his two hands up as he shouted Hallelujah. "How come?" He inquired. "It must be a divine arrangement," the Pastor responded. "Divine arr-an-ge-me-nt?" Tracy soliloquized.

"This will be the highest Honour of my life," she asserted.

She couldn't believe her ears. "Sir," she said after a long pause, "Please do not announce to the whole church that the Bishop will be preaching at our wedding." "Why?" the Pastor asked.

"Because we will not be able to handle the crowd," she replied.

"This is a divine arrangement, born of God for "whatever is born of God is victorious over the world, and this is the victory that conquers the world, even our faith" (I John 5:4),"The Pastor reassured them.

Jimmy was wordless. In his silence, he just put his gaze on the Pastor. After some minutes he said: "May I ask, what prompted this HONOUR or should I call it embarrassment' He turned to 'Tracy and asked, "Does he really know us?" 'Tracy was blank. The Pastor smiled and said: "Quite well." He turned to Tracy.

"Your monumental gift in honor of your father's 70th birthday caught his attention when he came around on a casual private visit. I was just trying to show him how far we had gone with the church building project when he asked for the price of the gold plated lectern. I told him it was a donation. Remember I compelled you to give me the name of the company that sold it. It was then I had to introduce you to your absence. The second introduction was when Bro Jimmy sang a solo at the city-wide crusade in East Africa three months ago. He was so impressed. His first statement was: "This voice is an asset, who is this brother, where is he from?"

"I then told him about your relationship and the proposed wedding. Incidentally, he would be speaking at the city-wide crusade that almost made me change the date of your wedding. It is very unusual for him to accept preaching at a wedding especially when it is not a Pastor's wedding. His comment was: 'These two have given themselves completely to the Lord; the Lord will do anything to make them happy. I will gladly preach at their wedding."

"You agree it must be a divine arrangement?

Remember: "A man's gift makes room for him and brings him before great men" Proverbs 18:16.

"Thank you, Jesus," chorused Jimmy and Tracy as if it had been previously rehearsed.

"Please do not forget to send in your wedding gown to the wedding committee for scrutiny and certification. You understand that I will need to pray over it. I know you are members of the committee. I should be able to vouch for your sense of judgment; however, you will need to fulfill all righteousness so that we do not set any negative precedent."

With a broad smile, he looked at Tracy and said "I hope the date of your wedding does not coincide with your "Pink Days"?" Jimmy who was lost in the discussion ignorantly said, "Sir, the wedding gown is white not pink" The Pastor and Tracy burst into laughter over his ignorance. The Pastor with humor and equanimity pulled Jimmy to himself and whispered: "She understood what I meant."

"I am sorry I did not understand the codes," apologized Jimmy. With a tincture of humor, he said to the Pastor: "Sir, now speaketh thou in parables?" They all laughed. The Pastor cut in to say: "Thank God your honeymoon will not be obstructed." Jimmy laughed and said, "Sir, now speakest thou plainly, and speakest no proverb. Now am I sure that thou knowest all things ..." Tracy laughed, till tears lined her eyelids. She conclusively added; "Bro Jimmy and his old King James." The Pastor smiled.

Turning to Jimmy, he said, "Now that you know the sign of the times you should know what you ought to do on your wedding night. However, deal gently with my daughter Tracy." They all laughed again as Jimmy responded: "It shall be well."

The Pastor, however, added: "Should you have any problem, do not hesitate to phone me." Tracy remembered those "dangerous days" when she was seeking "surgery" from Associate Pastor Dickson. She smiled out of context. Jimmy questioned her, but she just smiled it off.

The Pastor came up with this note of appreciation and warning. "Bro Jimmy and Sis Tracy, I want to congratulate you for your almost very successful courtship ..." The phrase, "almost very successful courtship" agitated both of them. They looked at each other's face and then turned to the Pastor. "Yes, you are now almost very successful. You have not won the victory yet. Your testimony is not yet complete. Your images and integrity are still at stake. I am yet to be fully proud of you," he affirmed.

These statements brought sudden sobriety on them both. They stood before the Pastor as if standing before a judge. The serenity of the environment undoubtedly negated the imaginations in their flustered souls. The seriousness of the Pastor was very imposing and overwhelming. There was no doubt every statement received the backing of the Holy Spirit. He cautioned: "You are now about to enter into the most dangerous part of your courtship (the last few days before your wedding). I appreciate your love for each other and the ever increasing desire for togetherness. If you are not very careful, the devil may destroy your testimony before the 30th of September. You must, therefore, be sober and vigilant because your adversary the devil is ready to devour." He turned to Tracy with a very stern look and said: "If you must maintain your integrity and win his regards for life, you must retain and maintain it from now. Keep yourself pure."

Jimmy expected the Pastor to charge him too, but the Pastor did not give him any personal caution. In his heart, he felt the Pastor implied that he (Jimmy) is the one the devil may use to cause any defilement before the wedding day. He determined not to visit Tracy's house or allow her into his own until after the wedding.

The Pastor closed the meeting with a fairly lengthy "sermon prayer." As the would-be couple departed he charged them again: "KEEP YOURSELVES PURE. This is the secret of a joyous, successful and glorious wedding day."

CHAPTER TWELVE

THE WEDDING DAY

What makes news may not necessarily be new. It is the freshness of the incident or information and the objects or subjects involved that actually make the news. The proposed wedding of Tracy and Jimmy was the latest, and much talked about issue among the Christians in Dakkoma City. It was such good news that successfully shielded off the facts and rumor peddled on the Scandalous act of Associate Pastor Dickson.

Everybody was eager to attend the wedding, more especially, the wedding reception. They wanted to listen to the TOAST. It was a common belief that the secret of convictions of the newly wedded form a major part of the toast.

Elizabeth, the dress- maker, was more excited than anyone else. She felt privileged to be commissioned to sew the wedding gown for Tracy's wedding. She determined to put the fullest of her prowess into sewing this unique wedding gown. It was going to be an avenue for her to show to the world what she had to offer. She was more concerned about future prospects than the initial profit on "building" a "one-in-town" snow-white wedding garment for Tracy. She resolved to seize the opportunity to probe Tracy's mind on issues relating to the conviction for a suitor. This was an area where she was facing what looked like the challenge of her life. Elizabeth was in her late twenties and had had proposals for courtship from four Christian brothers simultaneously. She was perplexed and terrified especially by the affirmative ways some of the prospective suitors presented their "convictions" She determined to share her plight with Tracy.

Tracy called at Liz's garment factory to pick up the flowing gown of her dream. She was captivated by the charming smile on the face of Elizabeth who had just completed the desired garment of the century. "You are very much welcome," said Elizabeth. "Thank you," responded Tracy. "It's all set, ready for you to confirm our perfect touch in the manufacture of wedding gowns. Come and see," asserted Elizabeth.

Tracy followed her, beaming with blissful smiles. The garment was wonderfully beautiful. Tracy inspected it with every care to make sure it met the required standards as laid down by the church. Her inspection was of concern to Elizabeth. She was not aware of all the requirements of a wedding garment in A-Z Holiness Church.

She proudly said: "The materials used are of the best quality available in Europe." "It should be," replied Tracy, nodding her head in approval. She went on: "I was going to be sure that my treasured body is not unduly exposed but exclusively preserved for my darling Bro Jimmy." They both laughed.

I am particularly concerned because a brother once told me that I was not a virgin in its fullness because he had once accidentally been able to view my cleavage. Since then I determined that such an accident will not repeat itself. Not especially on my wedding day when many eyes will focus on me. I have decided not to be a stumbling block to the coming generation. Remember the statement of Our Lord Jesus Christ in Matt. 18: 6. : "but whoever causes one of these little ones who believe in Me to stumble and sin [by leading him away from My teaching], it would be better for him to have a heavy millstone [as large as one turned by a donkey] hung around his neck and to be drowned in the depth of the sea."
MATTHEW 18:6 AMP

Elizabeth with the tincture of a smile said: "You can trust that our job here meets your specifications," she asserted. It was a good time for her to ask her inquisitions. She said: "Sis Tracy, may I ask you one or two questions?" "Please do," she responded gracefully.

"Please kindly explain how you came about having Bro Jimmy as your prospective husband." Tracy smiled as she confidently narrated the story of her conviction. Elizabeth ques-tioned further: "May I know what you desired in a man and why

Bro Jimmy?" Tracy had always been paranoid and apprehensive of any question that has to do with the very strong accent of Bro Jimmy, especially as this was her personal area of struggle. She looked a little serious as she answered Elizabeth: "My first desire in a man is the fear of God. Other qualities or achievements are secondary. His strong accent is very complimentary," she added trying to spare a little smile.

It was evident that she was defensive of Jimmy's accent. Elizabeth realized that Tracy was not ready to discuss any issue that will be derogatory on the personality of Jimmy. She chose to ask only questions that will interest her. All her questions were answered to her satisfaction. Tracy closed the dialogue with this statement: "My beloved sister, your best bet should be the Lord's perfect will. Seek His face continually; it is not impossible that the Lord's perfect will for your life is yet to come. However, if he is one of these four men that have shown interest or "conviction," he shall stand the test of time. Do not commit yourself to any of them until you have prayed through. Please make sure that you inform the marriage committee in your local church.

Marriage committee! She exclaimed. Interes-tingly, one of the four brothers is the son of the son of a member of the marriage committee. Another of them is the son of one of the Associate pastors. I very much feel I am in a fix." Tracy at this juncture promised to join her in regular prayers until the riddle is resolved.

She, however, counseled her to share her experience with her pastor or his wife if she feels safe to do so. She affirmatively said: "This is one of the most crucial moments of your life. You cannot afford to handle it with levity, sentiment or emotional infatuation. Elizabeth determined to share her challenges with her pastor.

They parted with a short prayer said by Tracy.

To Jimmy and Tracy, the twenty-four hours in a day were too short to accomplish all they had up their sleeves. They had a lot of running around to do. The brethren from the church were of tremendous support to ease them of some of the burdens. Everything seemed to work out well. The news of improvement in the health of Tracy's dad served as a great impetus. He was to arrive in Dakkoma City a week before the wedding. Jimmy's mother was booked on the same flight as Tracy's mum. His father determined not to attend a church service on any account. His adamancy widened the distance between him and his only son (Jimmy). Tenacious adherence to Islamic fundamentalism became very offensive to Mrs. Davise. She felt any religion that will not allow her to attend the wedding of her only son could be done away with.

Mrs. Jackson and Mrs. Davise were warmly received at the Dakkoma Airport by their children including the twins and their father who had arrived a few days earlier. Jimmy's mum was very impressed by Tracy's warm traditional style of greetings in the midst of a busy crowd at the Airport. She felt highly honored, but a little embarrassed as all eyes focused on her. She looked the most dignified person around, especially because Tracy did not' greet her parents in like manner. She only embraced them with a gesture of respect. This first impression swept Jimmy's mum off balance. She fell in love with Tracy. She lifted her up and said, "May the Lord honor you my wife and my daughter" (which implied my daughter-in-law). Jimmy and Tracy gazed at each other with smiles that seemed to say: "Parental Exchange." It was a good way to begin a family union.

It was Tracy's determination to win her mother-in-law completely over to the Lord Jesus Christ. Her love eroded every preconceived negative impression or intention Mrs. Davise could have had. To her, she had found the most lovable daughter-in-law of her dream. Jimmy was very impressed by the relationship between his mother and Tracy. His expressions were of excitement. He was very radiant and full of life. His exuberance was at the moment curtailed by Tracy's statement: "Thank God mummy (with a gesture towards

Jimmy's mum) is around for this wedding with more than enough milk to keep us going." She sounded a little sarcastic but was received with laughter from every quarter especially Jimmy's mum, who humorously said "Thank God I got two big tanks ready to feed one more child." She cuddled Tracy. "You will know I am a big eater," responded Tracy. Everybody laughed.

Everything was in place for the bachelor's eve and spinster's night fixed for 23rd September at the church hall. It was a time to share testimonies of their convictions and their experience during courtship. Everybody was blessed. Many who had made mistakes determined to put things right. The crowd was too large for the provision available. At this juncture, they were able to imagine the size of the crowd to expect at the reception on the 30th.

At the close of the bachelor's night and spinsters' eve, Elizabeth was more than anxious to share the resolve of the riddle of her life with Tracy. Tracy herself was eager to hear the testimony or answers to her prayers. She embraced Tracy with tears of Joy. "You are my angel. I thank God for the opportunity to meet with you. I am sure there are other dressmakers in your local church and more-so in the entire city of Dakkoma. God did not lead you to request for our services at Lizzy garment factory but to bail me out of my predicament." Tracy in her anxiety and eagerness to hear what exactly happened before her fiancé would interrupt them demanded that Elizabeth should quickly give her the desired information. "My pastor did a good job. He got me to ask some pertinent questions from the four prospective suitors. He told me the ideal answers to all the questions. One of the principles he asked me to observe in the expressions of their convictions is the compliance of their beliefs with the word of God. He asked me to also ask each of them about whom they shared their convictions before they approached me to express their interest in me for marriage. He also asked me to ask for their readiness, which will be determined by their overall maturity; physical, spiritual, financial and material. He finally asked me to consider their family genetic traits and particularly their individual genotype, more-so the blood group. I guess I did a good homework on them all and reported back to my pastor accordingly.

The first thing he did was to nullify the two whose blood type was 'AS' and 'SC' respectively because I am 'AS.' He called my attention to the fact that if I ever happened to marry a man with the 'AS' or 'SC' blood group, we are very likely to give birth to children with the 'SS' blood group which will make them very sickly because they carry dominant sickle cell traits. One of the other two was of no good spiritual standing. He was very controversial on some key principles of the Christian faith. The final resolve was Bro. Nathaniel. He met every requirement but for his financial condition. He is still in school for his doctorate degree, and his parents are impoverished. I do not feel very comfortable with him because he may be very paranoid about issues that may hinge on money or my achievements." Tracy cut in with laughter. "What is funny?" she questioned. "That was my first line of thought when I came to a conclusion on my conviction for my prospective husband." They both laughed. Tracy was cautious about adding: "Every yet to marry a successful career, or professional lady should be sure she is not carried away by her success. In most cases, our success may always become a disadvantage." "You are very right, that was what my pastor cautioned me about. He made me appreciate the prospects in the life of Bro. Nathaniel. I am sure something good will comes out of his 'Nazareth.'" They both laughed as they linked her statement to the biblical Nathaniel. The Bible states in John 1: 45-47. "Philip found Nathanael and told him, "We have found the One Moses in the Law, and also the Prophets wrote about—Jesus from Nazareth, the son of Joseph [according to public record]." Nathanael answered him, "Can anything good come out of Nazareth?" Philip replied, "Come and see."

Jesus saw Nathanael coming toward Him, and said of him, "Here is an Israelite indeed [a true descendant of Jacob], in whom there is no guile nor deceit nor duplicity!" JOHN 1:45-47 AMP

Elizabeth humorously added, "...now that not just something but someone good came out of Nazareth, I believe something good will come out of Nathaniel? Trusting God that he is an Israelite indeed in whom there is no guile." They both laughed. Tracy led a short prayer session before they parted.

On September 30th was proof that God heard and answered all the prayers offered concerning the wedding. The weather was perfect. The misty morning gave way to a radiant, bright sky that flushed the cloud with golden rays of the sun, friendly and graceful enough to desire to bask in. The number of cars called for attention. There was a serious parking problem. It was jam-packed traffic around the church.

The bride and groom were already in the church at least fifteen minutes before the 12.00 noontime. It was the practice of A-Z Holiness Church to start every wedding programme at the stipulated time, irrespective of the promptness or lateness of the bride or groom. Every "would-be married" had always been strictly instructed to be in the church at least fifteen minutes before the time. The idea was to instill discipline in the new home. Somebody once said, "If you cannot sacrifice all it takes to get everything right on your wedding day, when will you ever get it right? It will be too bad to start a home on the path of conflict."

The wedding was one of the most elegant and well attended weddings ever conducted in Dakkoma City. The sermon was brief but loaded. It was titled:

"The Bride of Christ." About two hundred people (including Jimmy's mum) answered the altar call in the surrender of their lives to the Lordship of Jesus Christ. It was an awesome moment. Jimmy and Tracy saw the saved souls as the best of all wedding gifts they could have received. It was their day of honor. Tracy walked the isles of the church hooked to the left side of Jimmy as they sang the recessional hymn. They were followed by the immaculately dressed bridal trail. The parents and the ministers followed them as they took their "first walk" together before the mammoth crowd.

Mr. & Mrs. Jackson were the happiest parents around. Their joy was full. It was a dream come true. Mrs. Davise (Jimmy's Mum) felt very lonely as she walked along without her husband. Her consolation was her new-found love and faith in Christ. She put her right hand a little out. One would wonder whether she was holding to an invisible husband. Her gesture was to suggest her first walk with Jesus, a Walk she determined will never end.

The reception was very glorious and colorful. The toast was very informative and inspiring. The occasion was chaired by the Mayor of Dakkoma City. The "MC" [Master of Ceremony] humorously said; "It is time to ask the question that has been kept on hold for the past few months. I hope I have the backing of the Pastor to ask our beloved Bro. Jimmy a question that I believe the Pastor would have asked

me to ask him on his behalf right now." He went
further. "Bro Jimmy, remember I was there when you
fell in the Pastor's office on that dangerous, windy
and rainy day. How did it feel when Sis. Tracy rushed
forward to pull you up when she saw that you were
bleeding? How did you feel resting your bleeding
head on her chest? Did you fall asleep?" Everybody
including the dignitaries at the high-table burst
into laughter. The pastor gently whispered to the
ear of the Bishop; "Sir, can you imagine how
observant and assessing people can be?" The bishop
responded, "2 Corinthians 3:1-3". Which reads:
"Are we starting to commend ourselves again? Or
do we need, like some [false teachers], letters of
recommendation to you or from you? [No!]You are
our letter [of recommendation], written in our
hearts, recognized and read by everyone. You show
that you are a letter from Christ, delivered by us,
written not with ink but with the Spirit of the living
God, not on tablets of stone but on tablets of human
hearts."2 CORINTHIANS 3:1-3 AMP

With a wide smile Bro. Jimmy's baritone voice
rented the air, he said: "You watched the drama for
free; I guess the fee will today be deducted from your
pay." Everybody laughed again.

"Well, back to your question. "Her embrace
woke me up, kept me alive, I guess the positioning
of my head granted me a speedy recovery.
Probably it was a therapy exclusively reserved for
the 'near-dead.' Laughter and extended smiles
became contagious. He went on: "It was a moment

to suppress 'the buttons.'" Looking at the direction of the Pastor, he said: "I guess I now have the right to press all the buttons." Laughter erupted as the Pastor and the Bishop nodded their heads in approval. It was a magnificent experience for the newly-wedded.

In his vote of thanks, Jimmy expressed his appreciation of everyone present. As usual, his very unique voice caught the rapt attention of everybody in the beautiful but jam-packed hall. He closed his short speech with this note: "This is our most glorious day ever. However, there is yet one more to come when we shall be the wedded bride of Christ. My prayer is that we shall all be counted worthy to be there." He was very emotional when he tearfully said, "My father, Chief Hammed Davise is not here today, my most desired gift from the Lord is the salvation of his soul. I pray he will be at the heavenly reception." There was unison in the amen that re-echoed in the hall. His mother determined to prayerfully work on her husband for the salvation of his soul.

It was an awkward moment for Mr. & Mrs. Jackson when they saw Tracy's eyes drenched in tears and her facial makeup messed up as she waved them good-bye after the reception. The old couple (Mr. and Mrs. Jackson) embraced each other as tears of joy rolled down their cheeks. Tracy's father mumbled, "Bye my "T," take care of yourself.

Surely the Lord will be with you and make you fruitful without any delay in Jesus mighty name." His passionate plea and prayers caused Tracy to sob. All eyes focused on the well-decorated Mercedes Benz as the newly-wedded were driven off to their honeymoon.

Jimmy wiped the tears off his bride's face as he said, "You are in safe hands." His kisses were electrifying, his embrace gratifying. It was a busy and bloody night as Jimmy had to do the much anticipated "surgery." The "TREASURE VAULT" was successfully commissioned. They both slept like newborn babies. Tracy was woken up with very romantic HAPPY 33rd Birthday kisses the following morning, the 1st of October. It was the beginning of a lifelong journey, a blissful and passionate relationship.

ABOUT THE AUTHOR

Pastor Adesola A. Okonrende is a product of the marriage between Henrietta Ojuolape (nee Adeseolu) and Samuel A. Okonrende both of blessed memory.

To his mother he was a boy with potentials but to his father a "Nazareth" from whom nothing good could come out. His mother was a very determined and courageous woman who believed that 'the greatest asset a parent could give a child is good moral up-bringing and appreciable sound education.' She was principally responsible for his (Ade's) education. Her slogan was: "You must love and respect your father irrespective of his lack of concern for your future."

This salient plea of his mother served as a great impetus to his zeal for the well-being of his father, who was well taken care of till his death at the age of 93 years.

Pastor Ade Okonrende holds a Bachelor of Arts degree [Fine Art-Graphics], University of Ife, Ile-lfe, Nigeria and PGD Theology, CRBC London.

Pastor Ade Okonrende gave his life to Jesus on 23rd May 1977. He is a full-time minister in The Redeemed Christian Church of God. He is also the visionary of 'The Chosen Generation Family Issues", a vision that has blessed many homes.

He is happily married to "the most dynamic woman," Pastor Grace Okonrende. They are blessed with four beautiful children, Grace, Chosen, Choice, and Royal.

Note: Do not write off a child. If you have to lose your hair to care for your heir, it worth's the salt.

Decision Page

I want to invite you to make Jesus your Lord and personal savior if you have not done so. Boycott Hell and embrace eternal life given through believing in Jesus as your Lord and personal savior. Prayer and fasting will not work if you do not belong to the kingdom of God, and if you don't with sincerity of heart declare for Jesus. If today, you agree to give your life to Jesus, the sample prayer below will change your life and relationship for the better. God is the author of marriage; He will give you the best of it.

Please pray:
Dear Jesus, I believe you died for me and that you rose again on the third day. I confess to you that I am a sinner and that I need your love and forgiveness. Come into my life, forgive my sins, and turn my life around. With my mouth I confess that you are the son of God. In my heart I believe that God raised you from the dead. I declare that you are my Lord and Master. Thank You Jesus. From today, help me to walk in your peace, love, forgiveness and joy forever.
Signed: _____

Date: _____

Call for counseling or ministration
Contact me at: 832-723-8470

Other books by author

ORDER YOUR COPIES NOW!

*Available at: Amazon.com
*choiceworldpublishers.com
832-723-8470; 832-372-0860

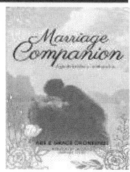

Notes

_____

_____

_____

_____

_____

_____

_____

_____

_____

_____

_____

_____

_____

_____

_____

_____

_____

_____

_____

_____

_____

Made in the USA
Columbia, SC
05 November 2020